"We are so lucky to have Santa Molir
Through Darkness as a resource for he.
sexual abuse. She reminds us of the amazing possibility of wellness,
and even more importantly, wholeness, that can exist for those
of us who have experienced trauma. Santa's story – and ability to
carry us with her through her journey as an immigrant, a child of
immigrants, and a daughter within a dysfunctional family system
– helps us to understand the complexities of healing from multiple
traumas and the systems that support harm much more broadly.
Her story is both unique and holds connections and lessons for
anyone that is interested in learning that healing from trauma is
possible!"

Cat Fribley
Resource Sharing Project Director,
Iowa Coalition Against Sexual Assault

Praise

"Santa is a gifted healer and educator. She can take complex, emotionally charged concepts and make them accessible and approachable. Santa's warmth and compassion comes through in all her work."

Kris Bein
Assistant Director, Resource Sharing Project
Iowa Coalition Against Sexual Assault,
resourcesharingproject.org, iowacasa.org

"It is a rare and powerful gift to bear witness to a survivor who has not only navigated their way through healing, yet who has also done so to the extent they can guide, support, and collaborate with other survivors on that path. Ms. Molina Marshall brings an authenticity to the conversation about sexual trauma recovery which reminds survivors that even though we may endure the most terrifying harm, we have a profound capacity for healing, for connection, and for joy in our lives. Her book is a compassionate invitation to be courageous about our healing which she models through her own story telling. Importantly, she opens the doorway to many resources for reconnecting with our body, our mind, and our spirit in this tender and necessary journey to reclaim a sense of wholeness within ourselves after the breach of trauma. Survivors will receive a message that honors the impact of their pain, while amplifying the enormity of their resilience."

Molly Boeder Harris, MA, SEP, E-RYT
Founder & Executive Director, The Breathe Network
thebreathenetwork.org

"Santa Molina Marshall is a trauma-informed therapist and healer par excellence. *Running Through Darkness: Memoir of a Spiritual Warrior* is a balm for trauma survivors. Using her narrative, many other survivor narratives and clinical expertise, Santa provides a compassionate way toward safety, healing, and transformation for those impacted by the scourge of childhood and adult sexual violence."

Aishah Shahidah Simmons
Creator of *NO! The Rape Documentary*, and the
2020 Lambda Award-winning anthology,
*Love WITH Accountability: Digging Up
the Roots of Child Sexual Abuse*

"In her book, *Running Through Darkness*, Santa shares her triumphant journey from sexual assault to healing. Her techniques, modalities, and tools for survivors and their families are insightful and inspire readers to tap into their own wisdom and unique pathways. In this profound work, Santa gives readers seeking renewal and solace a "safe place to heal."

Mary Pender Greene, LCSW-R, GCP
President & CEO of MPG Consulting

"Santa lovingly shares her personal story of healing from sexual assault as an offering of hope, while acknowledging everyone's healing journey is unique. She shares her wisdom while asking the reader grounding and authentic questions, guiding survivors toward insights unique to their truth. Santa extends to the reader multiple truths can co-exist, such as, 'healing is incredibly difficult and entirely possible.'"

Molly Chlebnikow, PhD

Running Through Darkness

Memoir of a Spiritual Warrior

By Santa Molina-Marshall, LICSW-SEP
(AKA La Cucuta and Rev. CanteWi)

Edited by Helen G. Morgan
Cover Design by Maryrose Snopkowski
Interior Design by YellowStudios

Published by

FROM TRAUMA
to *Triumph*

From Trauma to Triumph
Baltimore, Maryland
www.traumatotriumph.net

Paperback ISBN: 978-0-578-38315-6
Library of Congress Control Number: 2022904940
Printed in the United States of America

Dedications

This book is dedicated to the many people throughout the years who have shared their stories with me. Stories of sadness, fear, anger, and terror which are often transformed into stories of hope, courage, resiliency, joy, and happiness. Thank you.

I also dedicate this book to all the teachers in many different forms that have shown up to support, encourage and hold space for me. Thank you so much.

I dedicate this book to all the book clubs, reading circles and media outlets who support the success of this book. Thank you in advance.

I dedicate this book to all the organizations and particularly the *Sexual Assault State Coalitions* that have supported me and my work throughout the years, the *DC Rape Crises Center,* the *Iowa Coalition Against Sexual Assault, The Breathe Network, the Satchidananda Ashram,* and the *Kripalu Center.*

I dedicate this book to *Holy Cross Hospital* for providing me with the opportunity to teach not one but six yoga classes a week, and the *Sanctuary for Families, Inc.* for offering me my first advocacy/counseling employment opportunity.

I dedicate this book to Shameema Patel, Founder of *Leave No Girl Behind, Inc.* for her endless hours of support, assistance, encouragement and for accepting my calls and emails when I was overwhelmed with technology issues. Thank you.

And finally, I dedicate this book to all survivors of childhood sexual abuse and sexual violence. Blessings to us.

Gratitude

I give thanks first to Mother, Father, Everything God for blessing me through my journey.

I give thanks to Maxine Clair and Barbara Yofee, two beautiful souls who loved, encouraged, challenged, and coached this book out of me. They did it because they felt it needed to be read by many. Amen!

I give thanks to my editors, Helen G. Morgan, Nina Riley, and Love TaShia Asanti, for their support, endless hours of editing and encouragement. Ase!

I give thanks to Irene Walker for embracing, taking care of, and showing me what doing the Lord's work is about. Amen!

I give thanks to Maryrose Snopkowski who so seamlessly captured my vision of an incredible book cover. Amen!

I give thanks to my family and friends particularly my beloved sister Zulema, and my baby brother Yauki. And Denise Jones, Nina Riley, Dianne Smith, Sheilah Mabry, Aiku-Renee Williams, Roxanna Zachary, Carey Hicks, Akiba Onada-Sikwoia, my Ladota Sundance sisters, and all the other folks who supported me and believed that "one day I would write a book about my life." Blessings.

I give thanks to V for partnering with me through life as I grew into my awesome self. I am forever thankful and will always remember you as loving me!

I give thanks to the angels that just keep showing up in my life. Blessed be!

And I give thanks to my parents Hilda Estela Molina Alonzo and Luis Elpidio Molina. Thank you for my life and all that you gave me, even when you had little to give. May you rest in peace.

Note to Readers

Dear readers, please note that some of the names and characters in this book have been changed to protect the confidentiality and privacy of individuals. Some of these experiences took place over 55 years ago, and although my memories of the details may not be exact, I do remember what I remember – trauma memories have a way of being stored in our bodies and can be accessed with the proper supports and conditions.

Please remember that this is a story about trauma. There is content in this book that is violent and graphic and can be upsetting and triggering. If you find this to be the case, stop reading and find someone to talk to and/or consult a Trauma Informed Therapist.

For additional resources go to hpbysanta.net/links.

Table of Contents

Introduction

As a trauma therapist, the narratives, and stories of other people's struggles with Incest and childhood sexual abuse moved me to reflect on my own life. Among the lessons that every therapist, healer, and anyone working with trauma survivors need to know is that traditional talk therapy alone may not be sufficient for healing. Our goal is to facilitate interventions effective enough to produce healing, wellness, and the hope of offering a survivor the opportunity for a relatively happy life. Although many therapists understand and imagine the life altering effects of childhood sexual abuse, not many have shared from a personal experience, what happened to them and how they embarked on their healing journey. This led me to write a book that not only shares insights from years of clinical experience but also speaks on my journey of surviving and healing from childhood sexual abuse, and in my case Incest.

Childhood sexual abuse is a crime. Fueled by secrecy and invisibility of the victim, offenses are rarely spoken about in the family or society. No person or group is exempt from being victimized. Childhood sexual abuse does not discriminate based on race, age, gender identification, economic status, educational level, or sexual orientation.

No matter how we label it, manipulating, forcing, or confusing a child to enact or engage in sexually identified behaviors is an act of cruelty. Victims of sexual abuse are not only subjected to physical sexual abuse but can be exposed to pornography, forced to perform sexual acts, or be raped by a perpetrator. All of these are a violation of innocence, trust and boundaries and betray prescribed family roles and roles in other relationships.

Any sexual act committed against a child (minor) by an individual or individuals who have authority, power, and control over them is a crime. There are power disparities related to age, relationship and/or capability. Perpetrators can be strangers but most often they are known adults and/or relatives such as parents, aunts, uncles, grandparents, or siblings. Guardians, teachers, coaches, clergy, or any authority figure can sexually abuse a child. Here too, there is no discrimination. Anyone can be a perpetrator.

Children who are victimized are often overwhelmed with confusion, guilt, and shame. Psychological or mental abuse, emotional manipulation, and intimidation, often present in childhood sexual abuse, exacerbates the trauma of victimization. Some children are blamed for the abuse and made to believe they deserved or wanted to be victimized. Perpetrators may attempt to minimize the crime by suggesting that the experience was "not so bad" anyway.

The effects of abuse are monumental and can literally destroy lives. Offenses can be multi-generational and rob survivors of the ability to have normal relationships. Betrayal by individuals who are supposed to protect you can inhibit the ability to trust which can impact having a healthy, trusting relationship of any kind.

Equally alarming is the widespread instances of childhood sexual abuse. Twenty percent of girls and eight percent of boys will be sexually abused before their eighteenth birthday. Statistics show that the numbers continue to increase. Sadly, the number of children that are not believed or taken seriously when they report abuse diminishes the number of cases where assistance and follow up can be offered.

Running Through Darkness offers reflections from hundreds of painful narratives, I have been privileged to hear and the different modes of treatment that have proven to be most critical to my and those seeking my support. I include wisdom gained from reviewing an abundant collection of personal journals, books, articles, and handouts collected at conferences and trainings I attended and facilitated throughout the last 30 years. As the words for this book worked themselves out of me, I found myself flooded with my own memories of the fear, pain, loneliness, and narrow escapes. I took many sharp turns toward safety and healing that would become part of the journey that is my life. Instead of writing one more "how to" book for clinicians, I was compelled to tell my own story.

My desire is that those who read this book will be inspired to hope, to not give up on themselves and know that there are many different paths of coming into and achieving wellness. To know that no matter what they have experienced as survivors of trauma, they can heal.

And finally, this book offers a message to all who care about survivors of sexual trauma and the professionals they seek out for help and support. Do know there are many practices and modalities that can be useful to those searching for healing. The most significant tool, however, is within the actual survivor. I am a living witness of the possibilities of healing, renewing, and reclaiming that which has always been ours, our wholeness.

I do not understand the mystery of grace – only that it meets us where we are and does not leave us where it found us.

~Anne Lamott

Part I

1

The Beginning

*I*t was early September in New York. The cool breeze created whirls of leaves and made street debris float through the air. A small band of us from social work class made our way up the avenue to the 79th Street station to catch the number six train. In an unspoken way, we gravitated toward each other and stuck together. A current of excitement ran through the group. Truth be told, we were all a bit nervous. We chattered about our assignment and laughed at what we had gotten into.

I had managed to get into social work school while still holding down a full-time job at Sanctuary for Families, Inc. I liked all my classes but especially Social Work and Homelessness. For the second time that week, our assignment was to go out to places frequented by the homeless and interview them. We were required to write about our impressions by answering the following questions:

Who are the homeless and how did they end up on the street?
What kind of a life did they have prior to becoming homeless?
Did they have a life?
Did they have families?
Do they all suffer from mental illness?
Are they all addicts?

Professor Bradford wasted no time getting right to the business at hand. He told us to allow ourselves to be surprised and curious and to take note of our reactions and judgments.

"Let's hit the streets. Get out there and get the real story about the homeless population. Write a 1500-word paper and remember, it's due two weeks from now," he instructed.

My classmates and I walked and talked as we headed toward the train station.

"I'll have to wear a scarf over my face not to puke," one of my classmates said.

As we walked down the avenue, another classmate said, "Those homeless folks stink."

One of the guys yelled out, "Whatever you do, leave the homeless, homeless. Don't be bringing them home with you because you feel sorry for them or something."

Someone else said, "I don't know, some of them homeless people look kind of scary."

We all chuckled.

"Let us not forget, we're supposed to get interviews from them. Let us not scare them away. We need them. Don't laugh too hard yet," another one of the ladies said.

I reminded everyone that I was bringing food.

"I'm bringing some peanut butter and jelly sandwiches. Everyone likes a good PB&J sandwich. That'll get them to talk to me."

Someone in the back of the group yelled, "Girl, you better get them some McDonald's or something,"

We all broke out laughing.

We crowded into the station, some of us standing alone and others, in our school cliques. For a New York City subway station this one was well lit. It was the one at Lexington Avenue, an uppity station where the affluent lived.

Many of us rode the train to 42nd Street, Grand Central Station. Grand Central Station was where the underground world opened. You could catch the number 7 train to Queens or take the numbers 2, 3 and 4 trains uptown or downtown and to the Bronx and Brooklyn. In the early afternoon, the sidewalk in that area spilled over with Hunter College folks.

Some folks lived in Midtown and could simply hop on the bus. Although I was not crazy about my long commute out to Queens, I liked living there, particularly during the time of the year when the trees were just beginning to turn. On sunny days, the burnt orange, red and purple foliage was spectacular. Trees bursting with beautiful colors and layered textures.

Regardless of how hard they tried to make this station different, the garbage cans still overflowed. The stiff, heavy air still carried a stench. I made a note that this stop wasn't as pissy smelling as some of the uptown stations.

It was at that moment, as I stood on the platform staring out into the jungle of people, that I noticed a particular homeless man. There was something about the face of this man that caught my eye. He reminded me of a silhouette. He had the same look as other men who lived on the street. His appearance was disheveled. He was hauling bags filled with papers and fliers, the kind of papers you pick up at public service offices, I imagined.

There was something odd about him. I noticed his wrinkled black pants and the dusty hard-soled shoes he wore without socks. In one hand, he lugged a doubled up, brown paper shopping bag and in the other he held an unlit cigarette butt. The green canvas bag strapped across his chest was stuffed to capacity.

He had jet black hair but it was impossible to tell its texture. He'd put so much grease on it, if it were summer, the oil would've been dripping down his face like butter.

He wore a wool winter coat that appeared to have one too many things layered beneath it. What looked like an entire bundle of clothes was shoved into his pants.

9

I noticed that his pants were pulled way up above his waist and were held up with a very tight, wide, brown leather belt. His stride was what most pointedly captured my attention. His footsteps were poignant and prideful. He walked like he was going somewhere.

I was super aware I was supposed to be interviewing and learning from people such as this man but wasn't sure I was ready for the experience. I asked myself if I could really deal with people in the throes of homelessness. Before I could answer, I saw his olive complexion and black penetrating eyes staring at me.

I tried to look away but it was too late. My knees got weak and my mind started to race. It was as if we were the only people on the platform and bright lights were shining on the two of us. Time stopped. In a flash, I recognized him. This homeless man was my brother, Luis.

My heart was beating so hard it felt like it was going to jump out of my chest. I wanted to disappear, hide, and pretend I had not seen him. One of my biggest fears was about to come true.

From the moment the assignment had been given, I was filled with anxiety. The thought of running into my brother made my stomach flip. I wondered how I would feel if people found out I had a homeless brother, a brother just like the people we were sent out to interview.

Suddenly, he was standing in front of me. I was thinking, oh my God, he is going to recognize me. My classmates are going to find out I know this person.

Luis came toward me looking like the bag man that he was, begging for cigarettes. The closer he got, the more fears and shame flooded through me. What should I say? What could I do? Was he going to call my name? Would he hug me or grab me? How should I respond?

As I walked up to him, he immediately recognized me and with much excitement and happiness said, "Hey Manita! Hey sis! Cucuta!" (Cucuta – my childhood nickname).

I smiled to cover up the embarrassment I felt.

Do you have a cigarette, sis?"

"No Luis. You know I don't smoke." I said to him.

He did a grandiose turn around, a little modeling dance, belt tight, pants up, shoes flopping and waited for me to acknowledge that he looked sharp.

Luis was my eldest brother and it had been months since I had seen him. A few months before that day, I had run into him on one of my visits to my mother's place.

Luis was in his late thirties at the time and for about a decade had been in and out of mental institutions. He had been diagnosed with paranoid schizophrenia and often suffered delusions and hallucinations. During his psychotic episodes, he could be violent, disruptive, and oppositional. He often got into random fights on the streets.

My brother was not always like that. Luis had a good life. He used to have a lady friend. Carmen, with whom he lived along with her three children. As a child, I enjoyed visiting his house. They had pet rabbits. He had freaked us all out once when he told us while stirring the pot that we were going to have rabbit stew for dinner. This was back when he was normal. I remember refusing to eat the bunny rabbits. Who on earth eats their pets?

My brother Luis had been my idol. He was a musician who played backup drums and percussion for Eddie Palmieri, Tito Puente, and other well-known artists. He had come to the states and made a life for himself. I couldn't recall the point when he lost his way. The story went that, at one of his gigs, his drink might have been spiked with LSD. He never recovered from that.

The frequency of his psychotic episodes continued to increase and from time to time he ended up at The Manhattan Psychiatric Center, a hospital for the criminally insane. Some days he would dress as a Hare Krishna devotee. The next time he was a Buddhist monk or the President of the US. We, of course, attributed it all to his mental illness. At times, he would say things like, "Watch me make the traffic lights change." And as we watched, the lights would change. Often, when in the midst of a psychotic episode, he would have a grandiose attitude and exaggerated pride. He always expected to be treated with respect no matter who he was or how he showed up.

I wondered if my classmates had seen him approach me. Did they get that this was someone I knew or did they assume he was just a homeless person I was engaging with for our class assignment? My thoughts went to our whole family and I could hear my mother cursing this country and wishing she had never come to the states. My recollections dissipated quickly as I was brought back to the moment with Luis. As we stood there, I felt sad about how much he had suffered. Something within me softened. I fought back the tears that almost spilled over.

"Here's a few bucks. Go get you some cigarettes and find a place to get a shower," I told him.

"I will, I promise. I'm on my way to Saks to pick up some things."

We hugged. I smelled him.

"I love you, sis. I love you too, Manito, cuidate." (brother – take care).

As he walked away, I exhaled. I noticed that my classmates had gone on. I had missed the train.

Yes, Luisito stunk like so many other homeless folks who had not showered or changed clothes in who knew how long. But this one—surviving on the streets of New York City—was my brother Luis, my mother's dearest child.

2
Dominican Republic

I was only three when my working-class, Dominican family immigrated to New York City. Truth be told, I remember nothing from my early years in DR or the US. In America, my parents and their friends would often gather to have a few beers and reminisce about the good old days. They talked about how different things were back in the DR. Life in the DR—so they said—was so much better than life in the US. My mother in her floral dress and slippers and a face full of discontent, just could not get with the lifestyle in the U.S. She often talked about feeling like a prisoner in her own home. She complained of being limited by the language barrier and the geographical distance of everything.

"I hate being locked up all the time," she would say.

It baffled her that people just seemed to work, come home, eat, sleep and head out to work again the next day. That they repeated the same old thing, day in and day out.

In the DR, you could keep your door open and see the neighbors walk up and down the street. You lived like one big family and sat outside your front door and talked about what was going on in your life. You could be in your backyard, washing clothes and chatting with your neighbor. There was always something going on. There were people strolling by with baskets on their heads, selling fresh produce and homemade this and that. Kids would be riding their bicycles, laughing, and playing, free and with no worries. Those were the good old days, they would say.

"I miss those days when I sat outside my front door and could hear the calling out and people yelling, "Mangos, cuchifrito, agua de coco, dulce de leche," (mangos, deep fried cubes of pork, coconut water and milk sweets) my mother would say.

She never stopped missing her life in the DR. She missed the street vendors, her friends, and the open, non-confining experiences. She felt it was cold and lonely in New York. She dreamed of the day she could go home. She blamed and cursed my father for bringing her and her children to the US.

Supposedly, my father had worked for the government. It has been said that he was involved in politics. I remember hearing him reminisce about his work in DR. He did construction and painting work. He traveled across DR repairing government buildings and properties. My mother stayed home and cared for her man and her children. Later, she worked as a seamstress. I also remember my older sister Luz who we called Lucy talking about my mother doing other people's laundry. My sisters would say they did the laundry and mom collected the payment. Everyone seemed to have their own version of that story. Over time, the stories continued to change.

Although I remember scraps and fragments of those times, it felt like my life started when I got to the US. My dad had been a lady's man and spent lots of time out of the home traveling for work, having affairs and of course, drinking.

Isn't that what all Latin men do? My mother fought him but like every other good Latina, I remember her saying that she stayed with my father for the kids.

My mother suffered a lot; my father partied a lot. I also heard stories from my half-sister, Mercedes, that my father left her mother to marry mine. He left without providing anything for her and her siblings.

I could see her trying to track him down, waiting under a tree for him to get off work. She would ask him for money for her tuition and uniforms only to have him say he had no money.

Surprised and crushed, I wanted to reject the accusations made against my father. Not my father. Not my hero. I could get with him probably being a womanizer and having lots of women. Pops was handsome, tall, triqueño and machó. He married or got with my mother (one of my older half-sisters has since said that my parents were never married) when she was in her teens and he was thirty. This was common in Latin families—older men marrying younger women.

I remember one of my professors advising us, "I would encourage you all to go and find a therapist today."

At the time, I figured it was probably a good idea. I could see a therapist practice their trade and learn from them. Little did I know then that therapy would one day be an essential part of my existence.

When I began my studies in social work, a lot of questions were stirred up for me. Who were my parents, their personalities, and ways? What was their life like? How did they rear me? What went on in my home? I was aware that answering these questions could have an impact on who I would become, how I would view the world and my future relationships. Since my most intact memories began when in the US, I assumed I had been born into an environment where there were inconsistencies, violence, and conflict. I also believe these same energies were present in our home in the US. It was in the US that details from my early childhood began to take root in my memory.

My father and sister Lucy were the first two family members to arrive in the US. It was 1960 and four years later he sent for my brother Luisito. Shortly after that, he sent for my mother along with my baby brother Antonio and me. It was another couple of years before he was able to send for my two remaining siblings— Daniel and Zulema. My sister Anita never made it to the states. She died from heart disease in the DR at the age of fifteen. My mother often spoke about having buried two children prior to coming to the states. I found out later that I had another sibling who died at birth.

My brother Antonio and I were inseparable. He was a year younger than me and our age difference from other siblings had a lot to do with how things unfolded in our family. As far as I knew, my dad was very attentive to our needs. I knew him to work hard and provide for us.

As a matter of fact, the big issue I recall was his never being around because he was always working. I do remember my mother complaining about how he was always doing everything for everyone else, except us. I remember my mother going to work at factories and my many visits with her to the Income Maintenance Center, also known as the welfare office or the Department of Health and Human Services. Perhaps I was in a little bit of denial about my father. I was my daddy's little girl, the baby girl.

I can still hear my father cursing and swearing because my mother laid in bed in the dark during the day when she should have been doing something.

I recall him scolding and damning her for not opening the window shades and curtains and letting in the sunlight. I agreed with my dad. Why wouldn't she get out of bed? Why was she lazy and unmotivated? Why was she always running from doctor to doctor with ailments? My father thought she was just loafing, boring and had lost her groove.

At seven-years-old my hair was a big issue for me and everyone else. I had lots of it, very woolly and the type that gets tangled easily. Combing my hair was quite an event. The pulling and yanking and ending up with two, sometimes four moños, Dominican buns, was the style I could expect.

My getting a haircut was my eldest sister Lucy's idea. People thought of her as a woman of strong character. The fact that she and my father were the first in the family to migrate to the US and that her boyfriend was one of my father's friends from the DR, gave her some privilege and status. In addition, she knew a little bit of broken English. She was very opinionated and judgmental and had convinced herself she was the boss of everyone, including my parents. It was she who decided it was time to cut my hair.

I do not remember any particularly bad feelings about the actual haircut, although I looked like a cute little boy. When I think back on it, what remains is a sense of dread and sadness. My hair being cut seemed to mark the end of my being treated like a kid. There were no more grooming needs for me, at least not the kind that required love, attention, and care. Suddenly at age seven, I was a young lady.

There was another incident that registered as personal, though not in the same way. We were at the park for a family gathering and I needed to pee. No one thought to take me to the restroom. Instead, I was encouraged to go under the picnic table. If this was not embarrassing enough, my father, who at the time was very much into reel-to-reel filming, decided to film me while I was peeing. They all laughed as I squatted in horror. I was the big joke of the moment. I was humiliated, embarrassed and as though I had done something wrong, very confused. This film became a source of shame. My father would show this film when I least expected it. There I was under the picnic table peeing. I did not understand why they thought that showing this clip to family, friends, my peers, and even drunk old men was humorous. Although I felt embarrassed, the attention excited me. And so goes one of a series of contradictions which I did not understand about myself.

My brother, Antonio, was categorized as quiet and shy. I was considered the smart one, the outspoken one with the Big Mouth. These distinction between my brother and I was often made. I could easily manipulate him and I often did. I would talk him into doing things for me in exchange for protection, helping him with homework and getting other kids to leave him alone. I had lots of fun with my brother. We spent a lot of time together creating fantasy games.

My brother and I also played the traditional house game that many kids play. I was the mother and he was the father. We were doctors and patients. Of course, I was always the doctor. We would play with the neighborhood kids. We played spin the bottle and even pretended to make love.

We had friends that lived above us in the apartment building. They were a large family like ours and had two boys my brother's age and a girl my age.

One of my favorite games was bedtime. The boys would get on the top bunk and I, sometimes alone and other times with their sister, would lie on the bottom bunk. The rules of the game were as follows: the girls in the bottom bunk would announce when we were asleep thereby signaling one of the boys to come on down and pretend to fondle us. Sometimes I would continue to pretend to be asleep and enjoy the guilt-filled stimulation. Other times I would pretend to be awake and scold or hit them in the head and shame them for trying to take advantage of me. The rules of the game were clear, I was in charge.

There were many joyous moments too. We were known as the party family. Every weekend, starting on Friday nights, my father would start his routine. He would begin with the drinking and the playing of the old time merengues. My mother and older sisters would head to the kitchen and start the cooking. All the burners would be going. My father loved feeding people and showing them a good time. Slowly, people began to arrive, mainly men. The dominos would break out. The music would get louder, and the booze would flow in greater quantities. I loved it.

I still see the happy family that often went out to Coney Island for the day. I remember my family riding the subway from 84th Street to Brooklyn. My brother and I would be bursting with excitement. There was no doubt that when we arrived Papa would buy us hot dogs and pretzels and ask where we wanted to go first, that is after he stopped at the second-hand store and chatted with his friend.

I also remember going to Riverside Park almost every weekend. The adults would lie on a blanket and play cards, listen to music or chat and have drinks, while we kids ran around playing catch and hide and seek. The only worry on our minds was when our parents would start hollering, indicating it was time to leave. Then there was the yearly trip to the Puerto Rican Day Parade—a day of laughter, food, and many surprises. We never knew what colorful and exciting floats would be meandering down the street.

I recall those special occasions I got to spend time with my father, combing his hair or rubbing his feet for a quarter or fifty cents.

I remember staying awake in anticipation of my father's arrival. I'd wait up for my dad because I knew he would probably have some sort of goodies with him. I also knew that the dinner my mother prepared for him was much more food than he would eat, particularly the meat which we all felt our dad got more of than anybody else.

My father was not a food addict, he always had leftovers. I realize now that his drug of choice was alcohol. I guess my daddy passed on his addiction to me. I am today as I was then, an addict. My drug of choice is food. That's why I noticed he always had leftovers.

I loved my dad and his leftovers. I waited for him every night to make sure I got them. To give me a break, my mom would ask one of my sisters to wait for my father and make sure we attended to him. I didn't need a break and was always willing to do it.

I now realize this was one of the ways my pops and I bonded. Little did he know he was also feeding my addiction. The food soothed my soul and confirmed my Pop's love for me.

The beginning of the school year was another extremely exciting time for me. Not only did I get to go back to school and be in the learning environment with friends and teachers who liked me but I also got to go out shopping. Again, I remember my father taking me to the local shoe store to pick up my yearly pair of Pro-Keds and all my new school supplies which included: folders, a loose-leaf binder, paper, dividers, pens, and pencils and pencil sharpeners. I also got my very favorite jumbo rubber band that would hold all my books together. I preferred the big rubber band over a book bag because it exposed all my books and made me look and feel smarter.

Despite the joyous moments, games and adventures in my childhood, anger and violence took center stage in my home. My brothers were always getting into something at school. Letters from teachers complaining about them getting into fights, being disruptive or not showing up to class were common. My parents, particularly my mother, were often called up to the school. School officials did not have much to offer in the way of solutions. They offered what my mother perceived as threats.

"We will be giving your son Daniel a warning but next time we will need to suspend him," the principal told my mother.

My mother would fuss at my brother. How dare he embarrass her and make her waste her time. I can hear her saying her favorite words, "And wait until I tell your father."

I don't think anyone ever asked my brother why he was truant in school. I often wondered whether my father's constant drinking and violent behavior at home had anything to do with it. My father was out of control. He was always dissatisfied with what was going on. He tried to control what was out of control with violence, whether it was my brother's behavior or my mother's lack of motivation.

I questioned whether my mother truly lacked motivation or if her sadness or sense of defeat was a result of my father's constant rage and frustration with her. I thought my brother's behavior was his way of retaliating against my father's frequent whippings. When my father whipped my brothers, everyone in the home felt it.

My brother Daniel's whippings are engraved in my mind. My father waited up for Daniel and gave him enough time to settle in. Daniel immediately went into the kitchen to see what the women in the house had prepared for him to eat. He would get comfortable on the couch, sometimes high on pot, other times quite content with whatever he had been up to out on the streets.

My father would come and seemingly out of nowhere ask him, "Where have you been?"

Usually, my father had heard the news on the street that Daniel had stolen something or he had been seen on the streets when he should have been in school. Or he was seen smoking pot. Before my brother had a chance to respond, BAM! My father was on him. He grabbed him by his shirt and dragged him to the bathroom.

"Get into the fucking shower right now!" He would scream.

The struggle would begin. My brother tried to get away from him. My mother would plead with my father to please not hurt her boy. Me and my siblings were crying or hiding. I always tried to calm my dad.

As daddy's little girl, sometimes I had the ability to calm him. Mostly, I was not successful but I always tried. This was one day that I completely failed to calm my father down. I assumed Daniel had really done something wrong and that my father must've had a good reason to beat him. I watched as my father yanked him out of the shower, clothes dripping wet, horror in his eyes, knowing what was coming next. I was clear that nothing would get him out of this one.

"Stand there and don't you dare move," my father would say, as he swung a long switch, he made from electrical telephone cords.

"How many do you think you deserve?" He would ask.

My brother's pleas and explanations just primed my father's rage. One, BAM! Two, BAM! Three, BAM! Ten, BAM!

"You think you're a man, right? Take it like a man, you son of a bitch," He would say.

My brother stopped pleading and my father ran out of steam. My father would walk away, go watch television, read his paper, or have a drink. With his mission accomplished, he seemed satisfied and complete.

My brother would be curled over in pain. Sometimes his watered-down blood would be dripping on the floor. Why would he disobey my father? Why did he make father angry? How stupid was he anyway? I remember feeling very conflicted. I would feel both angry at and sorry for my brother. I hated seeing my father so angry and resented my brothers for provoking this behavior in him. I did not think my father enjoyed beating him or that it was easy on him.

I still remember how red and distorted my father's face would get and how he would have to sit and catch his breath after one of these episodes. This is the point at which my mother would come out to see my brother's bloody state. Mother seemed annoyed at him and scolded him for getting in trouble, all while wiping him down with a clean wet rag and patting his open wounds with hydrogen peroxide. Then she would use a cotton ball to dab on the ointment we called the red stuff that was supposed to help the healing process. I can see her fighting with the cotton balls as they would get stuck in the quickly drying wounds.

To my surprise, whatever it was my brother did to deserve this whipping, never came up again. However, this scene was a common one in our home. I should have known that ultimately, things would fall apart. I would come to look back on this time as the beginning of my parent's fall from grace and the beginning of my many attempts to run away from home.

3
My Brother and I

*A*ntonio and I were two peas in a pod against the world. The first time I ran away from home, Antonio came with me. Things had gotten so bad that one day we threw our things into plastic bags and left. I was twelve years old. He and I were now living with my mother in uptown Manhattan.

This was the period after my mother left my father. I call it the scandalous episodes of the Molina family. The details were that my mother left my father for a woman. This was the shameful stigma of the Molina family. After being married for thirty years and having eight children, my mother said she had had enough. She constantly complained about my father and rarely did I see them exchange any kind of loving gestures. His absence from our home became a major complaint. She resented him for being out of the house, always chasing some new gig or new hustle.

Her favorite saying was, "En casa de herrero, cuchillo de palo (In a home of an iron smith, the knives are made of wood)." My father was of service to everyone in the community, always helping someone with something but he was rarely around to take care of the things that needed to be addressed in our own home. She scolded him for not fixing this or that and for junking up the apartment to have the things in place he needed to help someone in the neighborhood.

She would say things like, "Go ahead. Go fix so-and-so's plumbing. Just remember that ours is still clogged. Maybe you can make some time to do that."

She also told him, "Stop bringing junk into the apartment that you don't need but someone else may need some day."

Dad was not your typical junk collector. He collected things he thought he might need to make something, fix something, or give to someone. To me, it all seemed very generous but to my mother it was frustrating and infuriating. She had many years of dealing with my father's junk and none of it was ever used to help us.

My father was a proud, handsome, tall Latino. His olive-colored skin, big mustache and dark hair created a striking look. He was well known and liked in the neighborhood. If someone needed something, they knew to come to my dad. He would either have what you needed or know where to get it. In my early years, I remember he had many different businesses. I guess he never got used to working for the man in the US. In the Dominican Republic he held a position in the government. The adults talked about his job as though it was a prestigious one. Yet, he worked as a laborer and a painter. I guess the prestigious aspect of his job was that he worked his own schedule and that he was his own boss. That enabled him to drink on the job. He enjoyed his booze more now than then. Drinking Johnny Walker Red, coffee and smoking cigarettes were part of my father's everyday routine.

In the DR, another thing that was probably considered prestigious about his job was having others work under him. He was incredibly good at delegating tasks because it showed that he wielded a certain amount of authority and respect. Here in the states, he had many businesses. In his take-out restaurant, he expected everyone to work. Yet, one of his favorite employees was a family friend called Gertrudis.

My brothers were expected to run around and perform whatever tasks my father decided they should do, especially since they had decided school was not for them. He, in turn, would socialize with the customers, have a drink—un cafecito (a bit of black coffee)—and figure out what they needed help with or how he could be of service. Then there was the carpentry store, the clothing and shoe store from home, the loan shark business, and the selling of booze. In the summer, he would organize the whole family and take us out to Riverside Park in New York to sell food and booze at the Puerto Rican Day Parade. Everyone would stay up all night chopping, frying, and packing all kinds of things for our day at the park. My father had many other gigs, these are just a few.

Except for running around when my father requested or demanded help, my mother did little. I recall that at some point she worked at a clothing factory as a seamstress but mainly she slept a lot and ran from doctor to doctor addressing one medical concern or another. To this day, I can hear my father cussing and shouting his hatred at coming into the house and finding my mother in bed, often in the middle of the day.

His favorite rant was, "Open the fucking windows! Let in the sun and some fresh air. What is wrong with you? No wonder you are always sick, always complaining and with all kinds of body aches."

Often, he would curse God, as though it was God's fault that my mother lacked motivation and enthusiasm for life or was chronically depressed—something neither of my parents knew the slightest thing about. One of his favorite sayings was, "maldita sea," (God damit) as he felt the need to curse everything, at times including God. I do not know how she put up with him nor can I imagine what it was like for him to walk through the door and be faced with the same circumstances, repeatedly. No wonder he stayed out of the house.

Still, my mother was an incredibly beautiful woman—about five foot three with a normal curvy Latina body size and shape—small chest, large hips, and big back. She kept her long and wavy hair dyed an auburn color until she died. She wore her hair loose except for the times she was going to the Department of Health and Human Services (DHS). For those visits she usually wore her hair in a bun. My sense was that she needed to tune down her beauty to appear in need of public benefits. Our many visits to the DHS office bring up another whole story.

I quickly got good at the DHS game. At DHS, we needed to wear the cheesiest outfits we owned, look down a lot, make little eye contact and act as though we had no capabilities whatsoever. My mother turned up her sad face, wore no makeup, not even lipstick and limped and moaned from the time we arrived at the door. I interpreted her entire demeanor to mean that a disability was required to get financial assistance.

Whatever little bit of English she knew, was immediately erased from her brain. I became her interpreter and assistant. Remembering the lies and stories we had rehearsed on the train was my job. I needed to make sure that the DHS office staff understood that all was not well at home and under no circumstances should we mention my father. My father would say that the visits to DHS were responsible for the beginning of the end of his marriage.

It was at DHS that my mother met the woman who was then referred to as the "social worker." Her name was Olympia. She visited the house often to ensure that there was no man in the house—one of the eligibility requirements for financial public assistance back then. I do not recall the whole story but what I do know is that my mother was soon paying personal visits to the social worker outside of DHS and the home visits stopped. My mother visited the social worker and my father ran after his gigs.

Then one day, the rumors began. My sister Lucy, who was the investigator and judge, gathered information. She had no concrete evidence but clearly knew what was going on. I hated to admit that Lucy was right but everything happening pointed to a painful truth. My mother was having an affair with the social worker. Soon after that or at least it seemed that way, my mother was moving out of our apartment and into her own. Yes, indeed, although she would never admit it, my mother left my father for a woman. Antonio and I moved in with her. No question that because we were the youngest, we needed to be with our mother.

Way before this, however, my regard for my mother had wavered. I guess I judged her for not being present, not being awake and available. She always seemed disinterested. This I did not understand. I guess no one did.

Who leaves her husband of thirty years and for a woman? Where did she get so much courage and energy? When did she have time to consider having an affair? She was always sleeping so we thought. I had already lost much respect for my mother. Not because she left my father, not because she left him for a woman but because she never admitted she was having an affair.

I would ask her to admit she was a lesbian. "Why don't you just admit it? You always talk about the importance of honesty and telling the truth. Why are you lying"?

In my mind her dishonesty gave me permission to challenge her. She had nothing to say to me. Why did I have to be respectful or honest if she was not?

One Monday morning, I was in bed half asleep in the room next to my mother's. The only thing separating our rooms was a curtain that hung in the doorway. Olympia was a regular visitor and often stayed over. My mother was still being deceitful and was still afraid to admit that she was exploring her sexuality.

Then, on this particular day, a strange noise woke me up. Instead of getting up and going to the bathroom to get ready for school, I rubbed my eyes and tuned towards what had awakened me. Why was my heart beating so fast? Why was I so disoriented? Had I had a bad dream?

As I listened to my heartbeat, I heard noises that seemed odd. I was sure I had heard them before in movie's that I shouldn't have been watching. I held my breath and soon realized I wasn't asleep or dreaming. The noises were coming from my mother's room.

Finally, I had caught her and she would have to admit it. She would no longer be able to say I was making things up and being disrespectful when I told her I knew she was with Olympia. I was okay with my mother being with a woman. I wanted her to be happy and do what she needed to do. I just did not want her to be a coward and a liar.

I often confronted her about what I had heard from Lucy and others. I remember her slapping me so hard and fast one day, I didn't know what hit me.

"You ungrateful one. How dare you talk to me that way after I gave you life and carried you for nine months!"

Yes, I was indeed disrespectful but really, I was hurt and angry. My response, which garnered another slap was, "I wonder if it was a desire to conceive me or a desire for pleasure."

Yes, on this day I was angry, when I stood in front of the curtain to her room. But even with a pounding heart, I felt a sense of victory. I had finally gotten her but I was afraid of opening the curtain. Was I ready to catch my mother in a sexual act with a woman? Was I really okay with my mother being sexual, period? I had never even seen her and my father be affectionate, not to mention sexual.

I gathered all my courage and swung the curtain open. Before I could say anything, there they were. Under the clean white sheets was my mother, Olympia, and my father. I could not believe my eyes. I stood there in shock. I was not sure if I should cry, scream, or explode. I watched my father butt naked, jump out of the bed and wrap a sheet around him. He ran for the fire escape. They pretended they could hide the act they had been engaged in. They tried to protect their dignity. I, still in shock, just walked away. Clearly, by now my mother had fallen far from grace.

Much worse than my mother's fall on this day was my father, my hero, my role model, and protector's fall from grace. Never had I felt so betrayed. I was angry, disgusted and heart broken. I experienced my first soul injury. My hope for a better tomorrow had been taken away. I asked myself, what was grace anyway?

Living with my mother and brother became quite different. The house was quiet. My mother was often sleeping or hanging out with Olympia. It did not seem like they did much—watch TV and sit around talking. Occasionally, they would have drinks. My brother Antonio and I were often left to our own devices. Thank God for Antonio. Prior to this time, we were already inseparable but now we really depended on each other. We played games, horsed around, and spend time outside.

We would often play Chinese handball against the wall of the apartment building across from ours. On the weekend, we would go to the local swimming pool. I remember us often going with a group of kids after the pool closed. We would climb the chain link fence, balance ourselves on each other's back while laughing, falling, and getting over the fence. We tried to keep the noise down to not get busted. No one was left out of the fun. We were at it until every single one of us got over that fence.

My mother did not seem to care much about what we were doing. If we were out of her hair, she was fine. Well, not totally fine. She did care if our chores were done. She was big on chores. She would often say that with children around there was no reason why she should have to do chores.

"Para eso es que uno tiene hijos," (that's what you have kids for)." She would say.

My job was to clean the apartment. That included everything but the bathrooms which Antonio did. My mom's job was to cook. She would leave the pots of food on the stove and it was up to me to fix plates for me and Antonio when we got home from school and clean up the kitchen. Although I already knew how to cook, I had learned way before we left my father, she never asked that of me.

Antonio and I had to do the laundry on weekends—something I enjoyed. Being out of the house and having something very structured to do that did not require my constant attention, left me with time to read a book or space out, which I did a lot. It was great. I also enjoyed strategizing at the laundromat—figuring out when to arrive before the crowd and claiming the washers. I would put a few items in the machine to hold them while I sorted the rest of the dirty laundry. I was good at timing things exactly right so that the dryers would stop just when I was ready to fold the next load. The hardest part was lugging the laundry up the five flights of steps to the apartment. Thank God for the handy laundry cart. It banged and scraped on the steps as I pulled and yanked it up one step at a time.

Once we told our mother we were taking some type of a drama/dance class at school. She did not know the difference, bless her heart. We would put on plays for her and her friend. We did a surprisingly good job at choreographing dances for them.

"Look mom. We want to show you the latest dance we learned at our theater class," we'd say to her.

I would dim the lights and pull out the red, orange, blue and white scarves we had collected from around the house. Mom had many of them for us to use to hold our rollers in place after getting our hair curled. The instrumental music would start playing and we would begin to dance. On cue, we would float around the room, sliding on the linoleum floor, leaping over each other, taking our performance very seriously. My mother would look on in amazement. You could tell she was impressed. Till this day, I wonder why she never participated in school parent/child activities. Was it her disinterest or did she feel awkward? She had moments like these when she showed interest. We would be at it for long periods of time, especially if Olympia was around.

My mother had no clue that we were just making it all up. How could she know? She seldom asked us about school, how things were going or about our activities. No news was good news. She was in a whole new life, hanging out with Olympia, chatting all the time, and watching television. In retrospect, I assume this was wonderful for her. She had a companion. She no longer had to be alone with the kids. She had an adult to talk to who showed interest in her.

My father may not have been very attentive, but he was certainly determined to get her back. For years and until he died, he never gave up. He would say that my mother was his wife and would always be his wife. On several occasions, he would show up at the apartment drunk, banging on the door and insisting on being let in, cursing her, and calling her names, particularly, cachapera, maricona and tortijera—all very derogatory words for lesbian.

I still remember the first time I had to call the cops on my dad. I would call out through the closed door, "Papa, please go away. Go home and come back tomorrow when you are no longer drunk. Mom is going to call the police on you."

What would he do if he got into the apartment? Would he beat my mother or Olympia? Would he just break things the way he did when we were in the apartment on 84th Street? The cops came, two of them. One put handcuffs on him and took him away. The other came into the apartment. My heart sank. I had just called the cops on my dad and gotten him arrested. I was afraid of what he would do if he got into the apartment, but did it warrant calling the cops on him?

After questioning my mother, while I interpreted for her, the police told my mother to go to family court and get an order of protection. This was the first of many times when I had to call the cops and accompany my mother to family court. My mother had never learned how to dial 911 and report what was going on. Nor did she ever follow through with filing a protection order against my father.

Antonio and I had less and less respect for our mother. My father finally calmed down and stopped showing up drunk and angry. I believe he finally accepted that his wife had left him. It was during this time that mother started going out. Sometimes she would meet Olympia at the bar right at the corner of the apartment building. Antonio and I would run up to her at the bar and ask when she was going to come upstairs. Other times, she and Olympia would be gone for hours. I assumed they were at Olympia's home or who knows where. She would just say she would be back. Usually, her announcement that she was going out would be followed by some order. Make sure you take care of this or that. She never seemed to talk to me, she just ordered me to do something. "Thank you" and "please" were not a part of her vocabulary. Children were not thanked or asked to do things – they were told, and they were not appreciated. Children should just be grateful. I felt used and disregarded. If my mother's intent were to make me feel like I was less than worthy, just a kid with no rights or voice, she succeeded. Was this all she wanted us for—to do the things around the house that she did not want to do?

Had Antonio and I just taken the place of my older sisters, whose jobs were to take care of the house because my mother was too depressed, sick or whatever? What was wrong with her now? She seemed to be simply fine. My resentment toward my mother increased with time. The more liberated and empowered she became, the less she seemed to care about Antonio and I.

My mother, to me, was a liar, a cheat, abusive, was really hurting my father and finally I had enough. On this day, I came home from school and as it had become customary, she was going out with Olympia. I cannot quite grasp the details of what happened, but I recall her commenting or ordering me to do something. I sucked my teeth in disapproval and retaliation. My mother hated it when I sucked my teeth. I might as well be calling her a name. But I did it often and this time she slapped me across the face and gave me a black eye. And after reminding me of who was the adult, she left with Olympia. That was the last time I slept at my mother's house. After crying for a while, and feeling hurt and disbelief, I thought to myself, how dare she hit me and then go out with Olympia. I decided that would be the last time she would disregard me and treat me like a nobody. I knew exactly where to go.

4

My Sister Lucy and I

y eldest sister Lucy had a big house on Clay Street in
Brooklyn. It was a three-story house, and she rented the
top floor. She and her husband Carlos who was also known as
Papito and their two small kids lived in a five-bedroom apartment.
Their children Andy and Lisa, then only three and five years old,
had their own rooms. In the apartment on 84th Street where
we grew up, there were four children and two adults in a three-
bedroom apartment. Looking back, it is hard to believe that we
all managed to have a place to sleep. Lucy and Papito shared
a bedroom, and each had their own office. Then there was the
living room, family room, dining room and an open area that
was used for a bar. All these rooms were filled with extravagant
(to me) furniture. There were couches and loveseats without the
protective plastic we had on our furniture at Mom's or on 84th
Street. The memory of plastic sticking to the back of my leg and
pulling my skin is still with me. And during the summer sitting
on a chair was a set up for guaranteed wet pants when you got up.
Even the kitchen table was covered with a clear plastic, over the
already plastic tablecloth.

My authoritarian sister Lucy had continued investigating
my mother. She sensed that my mother was up to something and

she was determined to get to the bottom of it. Lucy was appalled by our mother's behavior and her decision to leave my father. I knew she would protect me from my mother's selfish behavior. She agreed that my brother and I should leave immediately before our mother got home. Antonio and I packed our bags and off we went.

We used our school train passes to catch the G train. With my swollen black and blue eye, and our plastic shopping bags from the A&P with some of our belongings, we rode the train all the way to Brooklyn. I had ridden the G train before but not far out enough to get to the outside elevated areas. As we rode, I twisted around in my seat just enough to look out the window. Through the tears on my face, I could see the streetlights gleaming. Surprisingly, no one approached us or questioned where we were going. There we were, twelve and thirteen-year-old kids with bruised and bewildered faces riding the train after dark.

When I first moved into Lucy's house, it was nice. Her babies, Andy and Lisa were great to be around. They were cute and sweet. I loved hanging out with them and playing with their many toys. They had things to play with that I never had. Lisa had an awesome doll house and a great collection of little furniture and dolls. It seemed like they had hundreds of crayons and coloring books, puzzles and many story books. I loved reading to them and was proud of being an auntie.

Lucy had a television in each room. The one that seemed to get the most use was the one in the kitchen. She turned it on in the morning and left it on all day. Being at Lucy's was like being in a mansion. The windows were all covered with beautiful drapes. The floors were all shining hardwood and so was the furniture.

Papito was a stickler for cleanliness. Lucy was forever spraying Pledge and Windex, making sure everything was spotless. It was a good thing she did not work. She had a refrigerator, a deep freezer, her own washer, and dryer too. She even had an antique double kitchen sink made of porcelain. I later found out that it was over this beautiful sink that Papito broke her arm once.

Lucy took good care of all of us. She was always home when I got home from school. Dinner was always ready and she would have us come to the table to eat. For the most part, things were quiet and peaceful at Lucy's. Occasionally, she and Carlos would get into arguments and violent fights, but it never involved us children. As a matter of fact, Carlos was gone most of the time. Lucy spent a lot of time waiting for him. When I got home from school, I would do my homework, wash up and go to my room to play or watch TV.

On the weekends, we would visit Lucy's friends, go to the movies, the park or shopping. Of course, that was after we cleaned the house. My job was to dust all the wood furniture. I would use the feather duster first then spray the lemony smelling Pledge and wipe it off with a paper towel. The glass areas such as mirrors, tables and other things were sprayed with Windex.

Lucy and Carlos often had company. They loved having friends over. Dinner parties were common. Carlos loved hanging out on the weekend and listening to music while he had some drinks. He would sit behind his bar, prepare drinks, and play his albums. Their friends were extremely impressed with my level of maturity. I would help Lucy with the hosting and cleaning up. On occasion, I would even help her with the cooking. And if their friends had young children, I would watch the kids as well. Lucy was good at making requests and giving me assignments, just like my mother. Carlos was good at giving me praise.

Carlos was enthralled with me. He constantly told me how great I was, with compliments of my being obedient, intelligent, and beautiful. He also recognized that I could hold adult conversations and was a good dancer. He said he knew that unlike my siblings, I was going to amount to something. He would often tell me that he and Lucy would make sure I got a good education. He reassured me that I could become anything I wanted to. He was quick to remind me that my parents were losers and he could not believe what my mother and father had done. It was nice knowing that I was not the only one disappointed with my parents. He often invited me to stay up with him, even after the guests would leave and Lucy went to bed.

5

Strength and Resilience

My formal education ended in middle school at the age of fifteen. By now, I had left my mother's home, ran through the darkness that was my life and returned to Lucy's and Papito's home. By then another traumatic education was underway.

I was working at the local hanger factory from midnight to 8:00 am and attended The Spanish American Institute from 10:00 am to 2:00 pm. When I got home, I would do some chores, eat, help the kids with their homework and by 6:00 pm I was in bed. That was unless it was a night when Lucy and Papito wanted to party, needed a distraction or whatever their unpredictable requests of me were. At 10:00 pm Papito would be in my room and not for good or honorable reasons.

I enjoyed working at the factory. For eight hours, I was away from them. Plus, I was good at my job. I sat by a big, loud, hot machine with iron hanger molds. As the machine produced the plastic hangers, my job was to pick them up and pack them in cardboard boxes. I was fast and got a kick out of beating the machine. I picked up the hangers just as they dropped. I did not have to think, process, or wonder about my life, present or future. I could zone out and make up stories of love, peace, beauty, and joy. I would create stories about living on my own, getting an apology from Lucy and Papito for what they were doing to me. I daydreamed about having a family of my own, a family where respect and honor were important and a family where children were heard and seen.

The best moments were when I dreamed about being loved, in a relationship with a handsome young man who would respect and take care of me and take me away from the scary mansion, Lucy's house. By the end of the shift, I would have blisters on my index finger. I would come back from my fantasy world either by the ringing of the machine letting me know something was stuck, or the loud siren marking the end of my shift or a fifteen-minute break. Some days I did well. My speed was on target and my imagination was magical. But other days, I could not stop my thoughts or memories.

It was at this juncture that I met Mrs. Myra. She was an older, light skinned Latina. She had that grandmotherly look and feel to her. She was a sweet lady though a bit overweight. She dressed simply in long cotton dresses with deep big pockets usually with a wool sweater. She kept peppermints in her pockets and insisted on others accepting her candy offerings. I had no problem welcoming her peppermint gifts. Other than sharing her candies with others, she pretty much stayed to herself. For some reason, she wore nurse's shoes, the white ones with strings and jagged wedge platforms. She always wore gray or white sweat socks.

Mrs. Maya was not trying to be stylish. She wore no makeup and few accessories, if any. But what she lacked in fashion she made up in care and compassion. During the breaks, she would sit outside, eat her lunch, and get a little air. I loved going outside and eating my snack, usually a bag of potato chips and a malta.

I could tell Mrs. Myra knew something odd was going on in my life. She was curious about the man who dropped me off at work every night. She often asked me if there was anything I wanted to talk about and reassured me that I could if I wanted to. I did not know what to share with her, so I shared nothing. I always told her I was tired, had gotten little sleep. Or I would say that my sister was extremely strict and that her husband was very jealous. I could tell she knew there was a lot more to my story than I was willing to share. She also knew it was best not to ask for details or put me in a compromising situation. I was sure she had seen my bruises from time to time.

By now I had been at Lucy's and working at the factory for close to a year. One day during our break, Mrs. Myra asked why I was crying. I was so sad and tired. I saw no way out, no end to the madness. I could no longer space or zone out. I sat at my machine crying with the hangers piling up. I wondered what I had done to deserve all that was happening to me. Was God punishing me for leaving my mother's home the day she slapped me?

I had learned how to jam the machine so the hangers would stop dropping. This gave me time to catch up if I was a little behind. On that day, I was relieved when the siren rang indicating the break.

Mrs. Myra spoke a lot about God and referred to him as Jehovah. She was one of those pushy Jehovah Witnesses. The ones my mother and other adults used to say were a bit off. She had that look, the one you could spot a mile away. I remember when Jehovah Witnesses walked around the neighborhood or came to the door of our apartment, we would all get quiet and pretend we weren't at home.

This time when Mrs. Myra asked me what was wrong, I told her all of it. I was filled with embarrassment and shame but most of all desperation. Once I got started, I could not stop talking. She had no questions, she just listened. When I was done, she told me she always knew something terrible had been going on.

"I knew it. I just had a feeling. I'm so sorry to hear that. That is terrible and very wrong," she said.

From then on, Mrs. Myra became my confidant and angel. She offered to help in whatever ways she could. We agreed to keep talking. Over the following weeks, fifteen to thirty minutes at a time during our breaks, I told her my story.

I began with the day I left my mother's home at the age of thirteen. I told Mrs. Myra how I had left my mother's home and walked right into hell.

"It wasn't like that at first." I tried to explain to her.

But the horrific truth was, on many nights, when the guests had left and my sister had gone to bed, Papito had come to the room I shared with my niece, Lisa. The memories were vivid and even as I talked about it then, I cannot stop the tears. What a bastard Papito was; I was only thirteen years old. I was vulnerable, confused and in need of love and affection. He took full advantage of the state I was in.

He would come to the room and pretend to be tucking us in. It seemed like he was kissing me goodnight differently than he did Lisa. He would rub his hand over my chest which I thought was weird. I do not know how I knew but I had the feeling that the way he was touching me was not okay. I told myself I was mistaken, that maybe I was making more of it than it was. He did things like this almost every time he stayed up drinking. Papito had always been nice to me and treated me special. I did not think he would do anything to hurt me. Then one night, it became clear to me. Papito loved me in a different way than he did Lisa and it was not good.

That night there had been guests visiting. It was a fun party with lots of food, drinks, music and best of all, us children. Antonio, Lisa, Andy, and I could hang around the adults provided we did not get too loud. I was also allowed to help Lucy with hosting. For a thirteen-year-old, I was rather good at taking orders and bringing things back and forth from the kitchen to the bar. I remember carrying the traditional tray of assorted cheeses and Ritz crackers with olives and salami.

After the party, everyone went to bed. Lights were out except for in the bar area. Papito was still up, having a few more drinks and putting his albums back in order. This was something I often helped him with.

I must have fallen asleep because I felt the blanket being pulled off my feet. The tugging woke me up. As I opened my eyes, I thought I saw Papito run out of the room. I thought that was strange. But the next night, I woke up to him there again. This time he did not run off. Instead, he shushed me, as if to say, do not wake Lisa up.

I kicked at his legs trying to move him away from me. He said something I could not understand and then left. I remember feeling confused. Why was he acting so weird? And why was it so uncomfortable being around him the day after?

Papito was still nice to me and never made mention of being in the room the night before. This went on, for what seemed like weeks. It was days not weeks but to a thirteen-year-old, it felt like an eternity.

I remember feeling strange around Papito after that. During the day and when others were around, he treated me the way he always did. But at night, he acted differently. He scared me by coming into the room. He would touch my chest or kiss me on the lips. It felt strange but it also felt good. It made my insides tingle. Sometimes it gave me that intense sensation I got from holding my pee. I was reminded of when I played husband and wife with my brother and the upstairs neighbors.

He got even stranger. He came into the room very quietly and after pulling the covers off my feet, started licking and kissing my feet. I kicked my feet and must have hit him in the face. I called out for Lucy. The next thing I knew, he was holding my feet tightly and pushed them onto the bed.

"Callate," (shut up) he said angrily. "You're going to wake up Lisa."

He walked back down the hall to his room and I heard him shut the door.

To this day, the thought of anyone trying to kiss my feet turns me off. I still wonder did Lucy hear me call out to her?

It was several days before he came around our room again. I am not sure what changed but it felt strange being around him alone after that. He stopped being nice to me and stopped inviting me to stay up with him.

I told myself I was no longer special. Now I was just like the other kids. I wondered if Papito still thought I was smart and pretty. I promised myself that the next time he came to our room I would be quiet. I would not be afraid. It was not long before he resumed his nightly visits. I was quiet and cooperated and cooperated and cooperated.

I told Mrs. Myra about his many visits to the room I shared with Lisa and how over time, I became less afraid of him. I told her about the day I tried calling Lucy and how he later told me I should never tell Lucy what we were doing because it would break her heart. He promised he would tell her and help her understand our love for each other. He said he was going to leave her and marry me, get me a beautiful house like Lucy's.

I told Mrs. Myra everything. The many times he picked me up from school when I was at Junior High School 44. How he would meet me after school and ride the train back home with me.

I told her about the many times he kissed me in the mouth and around my neck and how I really liked it. I told her how he rubbed my private parts and asked me to rub his, how we hung out under the bridge in his car and made out. How he said he loved me.

We talked about my remorse and how sorry I was. How I wished I had called out for Lucy louder. Why didn't I keep screaming until she heard me? Why didn't I wake up Lisa? Was my silence my consent? I should not have been a nasty little girl.

"I swear, I never intended to take my sister's husband away from her." I told Mrs. Myra.

I did not think I would hurt her. I really did not want to hurt her. Papito was supposed to take care of everything. No one was supposed to get hurt.

Each time I talked to Mrs. Myra, I told her another horrifying piece of my story. I also shared my plan to escape from Lucy and Carlos' house.

I do not remember the actual class assignment at IS 44 – Middle School, but I had to write an essay and it had something to do with family life. Whatever it was that I wrote, the essay was a red flag to my teacher, Mr. De La Rosa. Through the powers that be, without my knowing, Child Protective Services became involved. Antonio and I became the focus of a custody fight between my mother, Lucy, and Carlos.

Mrs. Myra sat there in shock as the words poured out of me like raging flames, burning my heart as they made their way out.

I told her about one of the many times I visited the Manhattan Family Court. I had been there before several times as an interpreter for my mother. It seemed different when the judge was talking about my brothers. This time we were there to witness the process as Lucy presented and defended her petition for custody of Antonio and I.

A few minutes prior to entering the courtroom, a woman I did not know asked to speak with me.

She wanted to know who I wanted to be with. "Who do you think is a better parent?"

I had no idea that what I wanted mattered.

I told her about how Papito had been my boyfriend and Lucy was very jealous. I told her about how I had changed my mind and did not want to be his girlfriend anymore.

"I tried telling Lucy that I didn't start it, that Carlos is the one who started it. I was really worried and afraid at first about disrespecting my sister."

I even told the strange woman about the night I tried calling out to Lucy but she did not hear me. I told her I was sorry for what I did but I did not want to keep living with them.

"I don't want to marry him. He is a liar! He told Lucy I started everything. That I would stay up with him and insist on drinking. That I pushed myself on him. He did not mention the many times I asked him if what we were doing was okay.

He never told Lucy that I was really concerned about her, that I didn't want to hurt her or take anything away from her."

When I told Mrs. Myra about what happened in court, she was surprised to know that this was the first time I had seen my mother since that train ride to Brooklyn on my way to Lucy's house. So much had happened since I had left her home almost a year ago.

My mother looked different. She looked worried, anxious, and disoriented. In retrospect, I wonder what it was like for her to be in court fighting for the custody of her two younger children. It must have been humiliating for her to have to protect herself, her lifestyle, and her rights as a mother. I felt sad for my mother and regretful for what I did to her. I could have avoided this whole thing if I had just been obedient. But what about her, did she not owe me an explanation? Was she partly to blame for what happened to me at Lucy's? Was anyone to blame?

The question being asked was about who I would live with. Who was fit to be my guardian? Who wanted me? The details were a bit blurred but the gist of what took place remains clear. Lucy told the judge my mother was unfit. She told him that my mother was a lesbian, that she left us alone a lot and beat me all the time.

When it was my turn to talk, the judge asked me who I wanted to stay with. My court appointed lawyer, my CASA—told the Judge the things I had shared with her in confidence. She told the judge that I had allegedly been sexually and physically abused by the petitioners. I could feel my body floating away at that very moment. Everything went black. Why was she telling on me in front of everyone?

I do not know what I expected when I told her that Lucy and Carlos forced me to do nasty things which Lucy hated me for. What I clearly remember was staying in the court building as everyone else left—including Antonio, Lucy, and my mother. I guess I went into shock. I wondered what was going to happen to me. Would the judge send me to a juvenile detention center like the one they sent my brother Daniel to? Would he make me go back to Lucy's? Anything was better than going back to Lucy's. I kept hoping that the woman who told on me would keep her promise.

She had said that they would send me to a place where I would be safe. If I could not go home, to a place I could call home. I imaged this would be a place where I would be loved, taken care of, supported and nurtured. Not a place where I would be abused, used, and scared, like at Lucy's.

6

The Journey to Healing

I ended up going to a group home. The experiences I would have there would be seared into my memory. First, I did not understand why I was sent there. I was a good kid. I had not done drugs. I went to school and for the most part, I obeyed my parents. It felt like I was being punished for being abused and trying to get help.

I walked into the group home empty handed. As I sat outside the group home's office, girls came over and checked me out. Bewildered and feeling sorry for myself, I sat there quietly waiting.

"Mrs. So and So will be checking you in soon." the escort from the court said as she disappeared into an office. She left after that without even a goodbye.

The girls looked mean and angry. Seemed like they were annoyed by the fact that I was sitting there. I did not know whether to smile or look down at the ground. I avoided eye contact with them. The last thing I needed was for them to start something with me. I wondered where I was and what would happen to me next. I wondered if I had made the right decision at court. I wondered if I should have told on Lucy and Papito.

I could hear hollering, cussing, loud music and talking coming from what seemed like all directions. In my mind, I had gone away, zoned out, dissociated, and left the scene. This was something I had mastered by then. I did it often. I came back when I heard someone call my name.

"Santa Molina. Come in and have a seat", I heard the woman say as I moved towards the office.

I tried reading the woman. I wondered what she thought of me. I was trying to figure out what I thought of her, what I could expect. The woman was very matter of fact. I could tell that she meant business. She was not there to comfort me or answer my questions. She was only there for one purpose. To tell me the rules of my new home.

"There is no drinking, smoking cigarettes or pot or consuming any illegal substances. Do not open that front door. If you do, the alarm will go off. Everyone here gets buzzed in and you must have a pass from your counselor to leave the building. Curfew is 10pm on weekdays and 12am Friday and Saturday. Lights out and quiet time starts half an hour before curfew, so it is on you to get in on time. Whether you are in school, working or not, everyone is up by 6:00am. You are responsible for your chores. Check in with your dorm monitor for your assignments. She will also give you a weekend assignment for kitchen help on Saturdays and Sundays. The residents are on their own for breakfast preparation on the weekends. You are responsible for your own laundry. Make sure your bed is made as soon as you get up and keep your area clean. Your counselor will give you vouchers for McDonalds but you are welcome to sign up for dinner, if you intend to be here by then."

I listened to her words but their meaning was fading. I guess I was overwhelmed. I just saw her mouth moving. I felt sleepy and everything became quiet.

I came back when she asked, "Did you bring a bag with you? Do you have anything in your pockets?"

"No, I have nothing. I just came from court."

"I'll send you to the donation room and you can pick out a few things for now. You will probably meet with your counselor tomorrow and you can talk to her about getting some of your things from home and whatever else you need. You will be staying in room (blah-blah-blah). Dinner will be served at 6pm. I will show you to your room and the dining hall. You can come down to dinner if you like."

That night I slept very restlessly. I met one of two of the girls who reinforced the house rules and how things ran. I got a sense of who was really in charge and it was not the women who signed me in. I was not sure what or who was more intimidating.

There were girls drinking and smoking and having sex with each other, everywhere. There were frequent physical violent breakouts, arguments, and emergency meetings. Most of the girls were there for educational delinquencies, violent behavior, robbery and shoplifting and had histories of abuse. They all seemed to be sexually active and several were even pregnant.

The girl that I remember the most after all these years is a White girl who sat in a wheelchair. She had both arms cut off right below her elbows. She was pregnant and just seemed so out of it most of the time. There was something about her that seemed awkward. Her body seemed odd, like she had little control of her muscles and her head looked oval. Today I would say she probably suffered from Down syndrome or Fetal Alcohol Syndrome. But at that time, I wondered who would find her attractive? Did people like her have sex? I wondered if she had been forced too.

Memories of this time of my life seem surreal. I have a vague memory of where this place was. I do remember that it was near a park and near Columbus Avenue. I remember these areas as they hold stories I will never forget.

One summer night, some of the girls were leaving the house and invited me to go along with them. This was the first time I went out with them. We went to the park and sat on a bench and were just talking. Before I knew it, there was quite a crowd. Others arrived a few at a time. There were boys and other girls I had never seen. The guys bought a boom box with them and were playing it quite loud. They almost immediately started lighting what looked like cigars which I later found out were blunts, marijuana mixed with tobacco and rolled in cigar leaves.

This would be my first-time smoking pot. I got sick. I could not stop throwing up. My throat felt like it was on fire and my head felt like it was being stabbed with an ice pick. The truth is, I did not want to smoke. I knew from my brother Daniel and my father's many episodes that it was not a good idea to be intoxicated. But letting those girls know that I had never smoked pot was not an option, I knew that much.

They had already challenged me, saying things like, "You think you're an angel, don't you? You here for some reason, bitch!"

This would not be the only time I hung out with them in the park. We would sometimes go to the park after dinner and return before curfew time. These girls were wild. They were into boys and girls. Kissing, feeling each other up and even having sex, was nothing to them. I stuck to smoking pot, cigarettes and zoning out. That's why I came to enjoy pot as much as I did. It really mellowed me out. Thank God, they never insisted I partake in their other activities.

And then came the time we went out during the day. It was a clear sunny day. There were about six or seven girls walking down the street. I do not even remember if there was a destination in mind. Everything seemed cool. We were laughing, smoking cigarettes, and just talking nonsense. We stopped to talk to this older looking White man. Most of the girls were Black and this was significant because I was the only Latina. On this day, I participated in my first crime.

"What the hell! I can't believe what you girls are doing. You're kidding about this, aren't you?" I asked.

But before I realized it, one of the girls was offering the man a blow job for money.

And once again, before I knew it, I heard them screaming, "Run bitches! Run!"

And off we were. I wasn't sure what was going on but I was certain this was not the time to question anything. It was time to run and run fast. The white guy was running down the street, calling us all kinds of names. When he gave up, we slowed down and everyone started laughing. I swear, I didn't get what was funny. I was scared as shit.

Robbing people and stealing at department stores were a typical outing for us. I am so grateful that I never got caught. Another miracle, I lived through this experience without getting killed or incarcerated, as many of the girls did.

I cannot tell you how glad I was to finally hear from my father. Again, the details escape me. In the same way that I do not recall ever talking to a counselor about how I ended up there. I had not heard from anyone in my family since that day in family court. But somehow, I recall being in communications with my father. I begged him to come get me. I was uncertain whether I would be allowed to leave. I just knew that I needed out.

I sensed that I was in the group home for a little bit less than a year but it felt like it was a lifetime. There were new girls coming in everyday and just when I thought I had gotten used to the ones that were there, they left. Just disappeared.

So, when my dad said, "I'll come get you," I asked no questions. It is disturbing that I remember so little but I understand that given the trauma and drama I experienced, it is not unusual to have limited memories. I do remember the day my father picked me up. I stuffed a few things I had accumulated in a pillowcase and threw it out the window of my dorm room. I went downstairs and walked out with a day pass to visit with my father. This was my father's idea. I did exactly as he suggested and never looked back.

Whether they ever looked for me or not, I will never know. Once again, I was running.

I was saved again and that was really a miracle. I had not known how my time in what I call, "juvenile jail," was going to end. It was supposed to have been a way to protect me according to the family court justice system. It was a lot more like a detention place for juvenile delinquents. Really, it was a place for children to go when their parents fucked up.

Soon after I left the group home, out of the blue, my father, baby brother Antonio and I were on our way to the Dominican Republic. Only my father and God know why. I have often wondered if perhaps he felt like it was what he needed to do. His way of keeping us safe. His way of making up for all the other times he did not show up.

In the Dominican Republic, all seemed well. Although I do not recall much, I do remember it feeling like a Deja vu. The concrete brick houses, most of them one level with large cement porches, side by side. Our house or the house my parents owned was rented out to someone who seemed familiar to my father. I remember him showing up like he owned the place, boasting and being welcomed like the master had arrived.

Attached to the house was a restaurant with a coffee shop and bar area. I recall my father going behind the counter and pouring himself some coffee and asking a lady behind the counter to prepare two papaya smoothies for Antonio and me. We stayed up late, pretty much until they closed. We later found out it was our father's place; he had named it "La Cucuta."

There was a little house next door. It was like an in-law apartment. Turns out it was a house for the help or for us when we were visiting from the states. There was the big store diagonal to the house on the corner. You could get just about anything you needed at this store. I guess it was like the restaurant. It was a meat market, vegetable stand, liquor store, pharmacy, candy store, hardware store and of course a number running place.

I have a vague memory of going to private school in the Dominican Republic where I took some classes in English. Sometimes I would ride a bus downtown or catch a car.

The car was either packed with strangers or soon would be. Carpooling was the norm. Although I went to school as a student, I also helped the other students and eventually became a tutor.

I remember going on walks on the El Malecon or the harbor, with Antonio, my father, and others. Santo Domingo, the area of the Dominican Republic where we were born, was always crowded, and congested. There were people everywhere, on the corners, outside their homes and businesses. There were folks up and down the streets selling all kinds of things just like my mother used to talk about. There are lots of homeless people and even more homeless dogs and children. There are areas that are dirty and smell of sewer. I guess you can tell from my description, I was not too fond of it. I wondered what my mother saw in it.

What seemed like just a couple of months after we arrived, I recall my father saying that he was going to return to the US and Antonio and I would be staying with our eldest half-sister Rosa. We knew Rosa. Back in the states, before our parents separated, we had visited her home on several occasions. I remember her and her other two sisters and my nieces and nephews that were around my age. Although we had visited many times, it always felt like we were guests in her home. The idea that we would be staying in the Dominican Republic with her was a bit off. But what were our other options? It seemed like our father had none.

My father said he was going to leave my sister with money for our needs and would return for us soon. Rosa was not nearly as crazy and abusive as my sister Lucy but she was certainly not a comforting and supportive sister either. Rosa lived in the Dominican

Republic I think with her husband. I did not know where her son was. I guessed he was in the US with one of her sisters.

Rosa owned and ran a large hostel. I never knew if my father sent her money for our care, but soon after he left, she had Antonio and I working at the hostel. I remember her saying one day, "El sin verquenza de tu padre se cree que ustedes no comen," which means (that irresponsible father of yours thinks you don't eat). What she meant by that saying was, "You guys eat and sleep and it costs me to keep you. You'll have to work for your keep. Nothing is free. I don't know what your irresponsible father thinks."

From that day on, my exchange for room and board was cleaning the rooms for the residents, cleaning the kitchen after the cook and any other tasks she needed help with. Antonio, as was the case when we were back home in the states, was responsible for cleaning the bathrooms.

I am not sure whether my sister Rosa was fonder of us or the help but at least we got days off and seemed appreciated. I always felt like a burden to her. Later I would learn that she was as fond of us as she was of our father. The stories I would hear about how she and her siblings felt about our father got clearer.

Mercedes, the youngest of my three stepsisters, would later share stories of how inconsiderate, irresponsible our father was.

I cannot say Rosa was ever abusive. She did not hit us or sexually molest us. However, it was humiliating and hurtful to be treated like the help.

We were even limited to eating with and sleeping where the help slept. Rosa was not going to give up a room she could rent. She always reminded us that we should be grateful and that my father was a loser. I was grateful to her for taking us in but I came to understand that she only kept us because we were free labor and because she had no other choice.

We ended up being stuck in the Dominican Republic for a year, working as help at my stepsister's hostel. It was better than living in the group home and God knows it was certainly better than living with Lucy.

But after almost a year of living in the DR with no hope of returning home and no sign of my father, the conversation engrained in every immigrant came to me. I knew that as a legal resident of the US, you were not allowed to stay out of the country for over twelve months without risking losing your US residency.

Although I was born in DR, the Dominican Republic was not my home. The idea of being stuck there for the rest of my life was horrifying. I remember talking to Rosa about it and asking her if she knew my father's plan.

She, very matter-of-factly said, "Your father is still an irresponsible, shameless human being. Do you think he cares about immigration? Has he been responsible for you since he left here?"

I did not want to believe what she was saying but the truth was, my father had just vanished. For all I knew he could've been dead.

With a heavy heart and feeling very alone and desperate, I remember talking to Antonio about what was going on.

"So, what are we going to do, sis?"

I cried myself to sleep that night thinking, who could I call on? I had no one's phone number back home. I called on God.

God, please help me figure this one out. Please God, please.

The next morning, I remember waking up with a number on my mind. 718-389-0273.

When I realized who that number belonged to, I asked, "Is this God's will? Really?"

It was on this day that I made a dreadful decision. I not only remembered their number but I also knew they would take a collect call from me. I remember her saying often, "Everyone calls me when they are in trouble. That's why I'll never change my number."

I used a rotator dial public phone out in the corridor between two of the hostel buildings. I did not want Rosa to see me or know that I was calling home for help. The last thing I wanted was for her to think I was ungrateful like my father.

My heart was pounding. My face was as hot and red as fire. My hands were shaking and sweating and my head felt like it was bursting open. I did not know what to say but I knew this was the only way home. With each ring, my heartbeat got louder and louder, drowning out every thought I had, except for one. "You must be crazy!" my mind screamed loudly. And just as I got ready to hang up, thinking there would be no answer, the operator spoke asking if the person on the other line would accept a collect call from Santa Molina. After a moment of hesitation, the voice responded, yes.

7

Coming Home

I could not believe she accepted the call, but I knew she would. Then I heard her voice.

"Alo! Alo!"

"Hola Lucy, soy yo Cúcuta." I said quietly.

"Quien? Who is it?" She said,

"It's me Cúcuta," My voice trembled as I answered.

"What's going on? Are you okay?"

I talked fast while looking around and hoping not to be seen.

I told her the story about father bringing us to DR, leaving us with Rosa and never coming back for us.

"You know that if you're there for over a year, you won't be able to come back."

"I know, I know," I said sobbing.

"Stop crying! You always call on me when you are fucked. You don't remember me otherwise."

I realized what a terrible mistake I had made by calling Lucy but what else was I to do?

"Please help us, Lucy. I promise I will behave. I am sorry. I'm really sorry."

As I pleaded for help, I was flooded with thoughts from the past. It came back to me like it was happening all over again. What was I sorry for? For trying to take Papito from her? But what about what he did? And what about what she did? Why didn't she believe me? Why did she let them take me to that horrible place?

I was so confused and scared. I could not believe all that had happened. It felt like I had been brainwashed. I almost did not know what was real anymore. What I knew was I desperately needed her help.

As I was coming back from that awful trance, I heard Lucy saying, "Are you sure you aren't going to start that shit again?"

She must have been speaking for a while but I had not heard a word. Maybe it was better that way. By the end of our conversation, she had made me take full blame for all that had happened at her home and made me promise I would stay away from her husband and do as they say.

The next thing I knew she had spoken to Rosa and we were on our way back to the states and to Lucy's house.

To this day I asked myself why I returned to Lucy's home. Why had I trusted her again? And I would later wonder if it would have been better to continue working for Rosa in DR.

This is what I told Mrs. Myra. I had never told anyone all that happened to me. When I finished, Mrs. Myra had one question.

"So why did you go back to them?"

Her question caused me to feel immense shame and guilt. I instantly regretted telling her anything. I could see she did not understand why I would return to the home where I had been treated so abusively.

"I made another very stupid mistake." I told her. Despite all the madness at Lucy's, I knew she would get me back to the states.

Pops had left us with our stepsister in DR. He told us he would come back for us. Almost a year had passed and we had not heard from him. It was crazy that Lucy and her husband were the only folks I thought to call and the only people I knew how to reach. Another one of those times of desperation.

Like that day Antonio and I had taken the train to Brooklyn running from my mother, I had the sense that Lucy would be there and be willing to take us in. And even though I thought it was a mistake to come back to Lucy's, had I not made that call, we would have still been in DR. We would have been listed as undocumented and been stuck there, waiting for our father to return for us.

"I believed them when they said I'd be safe this time. Lucy made me promise that I was done trying to take her husband and I promised. Apparently, Carlos did not promise to stay out of my room. And if he did, well, he broke his promise." I told Mrs. Myra.

I was grateful that Mrs. Myra took time to listen to me and offer support and encouragement. She reminded me to have hope.

"Just don't return to them. You can find a safe place to live and get another job. Do not be afraid. God will take care of you."

Mrs. Myra was a little preachy. She was always talking about "God this and God that." She made it seem like God was going to take care of everything. And He did.

To my surprise, I never heard her cuss God the way my father did, especially when he was annoyed or angry. She spoke of God as a benevolent father. One you would want to tell everyone about. The type of father you would want to serve, make happy and please. She referred to stories in the Bible and often invited me to her church.

The invitation to her church came before she knew about the mess, I was in. She must have gotten paranoid and feared getting into the mess along with me. I assumed that was why she never mentioned my going to her church again.

As time went on, I became more and more comfortable with Mrs. Myra. At least she was consistent. She gave me hope that I could one day be able to leave Lucy and Papito's home again. I was afraid of being on my own but I was more afraid of staying where I was.

One night, during our break at the hanger factory, I made up my mind. I was going to visit Mrs. Myra. I would leave school right after Carlos dropped me off. The consequences would be great. I might get a beating, a scolding or maybe endure sexual torture and humiliation. It did not matter to me anymore. I was going to let Mrs. Myra help me to get me out of the hell I was living in.

I had no idea how it would come together. Would Mrs. Myra let me live with her? I did not know what to expect but I was willing to give it a try. I was desperate and anything was better than what I had. Somehow, deep in my soul, I sensed that Mrs. Myra was the angel God sent me, the one I so often asked Him to send. So, between her and God, I was going to be okay.

That morning I left Lucy's house like any other morning. I got into Carlos's car, and as usual, he proceeded to drive me to the Institute in Manhattan. My thoughts and my heart were racing. I wondered if he could tell that I was up to something. Things had gotten strange between us. He was no longer kind. Instead, he treated me like a liar and often said I was just "una puta (a whore)." We barely talked that morning which was not unusual. Little did he know this was going to be the day I began to fight back.

All I could think of during the drive to the Institute was my conversations with Mrs. Myra. I remember telling her, "If I'm not at the Institute when he returns for me, he will kill me or beat me so bad I'll be sorry I ever lied.

"You must take the risk." She had said.

I knew she was right.

The plan was for me to leave the Institute as soon as possible that morning and go to Mrs. Myra's. I had to be back there in time for him to pick me up and not let on that I had not stayed at school. I used to get beaten just because they thought I was lying. I could not imagine what they would do if they knew I lied.

After he dropped me off, I waited about ten minutes then walked back out of the building. I looked around and made sure Carlos was really gone. Oh, my God, if he found me outside the building, I could not give it much more thought. If I thought about it too hard, I would talk myself out of going to Mrs. Myra's.

She had given me directions to her place. I caught the #1 train at Times Square and rode for about thirty minutes transferred to the #7 and then the R and finally the L train.

Mrs. Myra lived in the projects in an area in Brooklyn I had never been to. I was glad it was daylight. I do not know how I would have felt had I gone there at night. Mrs. Myra was about four blocks away from the train station, it did not look or feel safe. I was so glad when I finally got to her building.

The moment I walked into her apartment, I noticed how dark and depressing her home was. There was an odor I could not identify and I could not help but notice how dingy and dirty it looked. I do not know what I expected but it was not this. Her home looked nothing like Lucy's where you could eat off the floor. Mrs. Myra's home was very crowded and cluttered. She invited me into the kitchen and asked me to sit. After offering me something to drink, she asked how things went that morning. I told her I was afraid but was glad to see her. Her dining room table was covered with papers and knick knacks. I even noticed a roach crawling on one of the chairs. I remember hoping she did not notice my surprise and how grossed out I was. But I must say I was glad to see her. We talked all day.

There was so much more I wanted to tell her but I was running out of time and needed to get back to the Institute. Carlos would be there to pick me up. That was his way of making sure I did not go out there and "fuck around," as he put it. To him, I was a woman now. If I was going to live in his home and be fucking other men, he would not be a punk and take care of another man's woman, without fucking her.

Mrs. Myra and I looked through the newspaper for apartments and made several calls.

"Start saving your money. Give yourself to Jehovah. He will take care of you." Mrs. Myra told me.

I did not know what that meant or what to do with it, but I wanted to believe her. I cried all the way back to the Institute. I slipped into the typing lab class and started typing away. Before I knew it, the bell rang and it was time to leave. As I expected, Carlos was waiting outside. I guess Jehovah did take care of me. If Carlos knew what my day had really been like it would have been hell. I held my breath all the way home. It was not until we were back at the house that I knew I was on my way out.

Once again, I have little recollection of the day I left Lucy's house. This does not surprise me. I was on autopilot, dissociating. Thinking about it too much would have been paralyzing. The move itself was simple. I had a few pieces of clothing, no personal things, or furnishings. I was moving to Jackson Heights, Queens which was a forty-five-minute train ride from Lucy's. Thankfully, I needed very little as my new space was fully furnished.

Out of all the trauma I went through, one of the things that remains stuck in my mind is Lucy and Carlos justifying their attitudes and actions. How could they not see how abusive and wrong they were. When I told them I was leaving they laughed. Where do you think you're going? Quien cres tu que te va a mantener? Lucy asked. (Who do you think is going to support you?) As to assess whether I was going to some guy's home, they insisted on dropping me off. As we were preparing to leave, I felt a mix of fear, relief, and loneliness. I remember their words when they dropped me off at the rooming house.

"So, this is what you want? You want to be a woman now? You think this is a better life?"

I also remember them flinging the word, "puta, mala agradecida" (you ungrateful bitch), in my face as they put me out of the car and drove away.

8

On My Own

The room was perfect for me. There were six other women living there. Each of us had our own bedroom and we shared the eat-in kitchen and bathroom. There was also a common area but I never hung out there. I did not want the women asking me too many questions.

I was only sixteen years old when I got my first place. I was proud of my little room. I had all I needed. A small black and white thirteen-inch television, a twin-size bed and night table, a chest of drawers and a small alarm clock radio. The women were nice to me. On the weekend, they would invite me to come out of my room and sit with them in the kitchen, have coffee or tea.

"I like staying in my room." I would say.

And I did. I enjoyed reading and listening to the radio, coloring in one of my many coloring books with my huge box of crayons. I welcomed the quietness and peacefulness. The weekends were my time to get myself organized for the week. This is when all those chores mom and Lucy had me do came in handy. Doing my laundry, going grocery shopping, cooking meals for the week and organizing my room were relaxing and even entertaining.

I was finally on my own. I thanked God every day I did not run into Lucy and Carlos. Before laying down to sleep for the night, I would get on my knees and pray.

"God please keep them away from me. Forgive me for whatever sin I committed. I swear I'll be good but please get them to leave me alone."

I prayed they were done trying to manipulate, scare and humiliate me. I wondered if they had found someone else to mess with. They always seemed to have a project they were working on which involved them trying to control someone's life.

It was hard to believe that I was safe from their torture and influence. The last time I had seen Lucy and Papito was that Wednesday evening as I was leaving work headed home. I thought I saw their car parked outside my workplace. It seemed like they always knew where I was. When I least expected it, they would just appear. Driven by jealousy and madness, I felt they believed that they owned me or I owed them. I did not know if I should run back in the building, run to the train, and start yelling for help or just let them beat me again. I was flooded with flashes from the past abuse.

It was as though I was looking at snap shots through one of those toy cameras. The scenes kept coming. Many times, I was forced to lie in their bed and cooperate. I saw a flash of the day he forced me to perform oral sex on him or was it on her that time? The day Lucy cut all my hair off as she yanked and smacked my head, on the bathroom sink, after beating me. Her being in a rage following some story she had in her head about me wanting her man again.

Flash back to the day Papito beat Antonio. I could hear him screaming. I prayed so hard to God that day.

"Please don't let him kill him. Please, dear God, help Antonio." I pleaded to God, hoping he would hear me this time.

I can still hear poor Antonio screaming and begging that bastard to please stop beating him. He punched him in his face then his stomach until he dropped to the floor. As if that were not enough to see him curled up on the floor in agony, he kicked him.

I heard him say, "Don't you ever get in my face trying to defend that bitch." referring to me.

My baby brother, only fourteen-years-old, skinny, ashy Antonio, my buddy, was taking a beating for me. I should have warned him that they had no mercy.

And then another flash filled me with more thoughts of Lucy. Her justifying what was being done to me under the guise that I wanted to take her husband. Her acting like what she and Papito were doing was an appropriate punishment. How could she be okay with the many times he forced us to be sexual with each other while he watched? And what came over her when she would slap me, pull my hair, and push me around because she was angry, or enraged at the fact that I dared bite her breast on a day when she forced herself on me. I could not believe I broke her skin.

Another flash of the day was them assuming my excruciating menstrual pains were due to a hidden pregnancy. Them deciding I was experiencing the results of being promiscuous which was confirmed by the emergency room doctor at Greenbelt Hospital. The doctor calling what I was going through a self-induced abortion. I could not believe this was the explanation the doctor gave them for my condition. I remember that day like it was yesterday. I was bleeding very heavily. At times, being on my cycle kept them from messing with me. But this day, they were annoyed at me. I was interfering with their plans. Papito asked me if I was aborting and had I been fucking someone out there. He insisted I tell him the truth. No amount of explaining and swearing that I was not having sex outside of the home was satisfying to him. Taking me to the hospital was a threat, a way to prove their point. I was not going to live in their home and be out there fucking others, he would say. I could see where he was going with this.

I just wanted the pain to stop. I had nothing to hide. The doctors at the emergency room would have an explanation and get him off my back. I was horrified when the doctor gave his diagnosis. Didn't he know that they would and could kill me? And how was it possible that I was pregnant, miscarrying, when I was not even sexual other than when Lucy and Papito forced me into sexual acts. They said I had done this to myself to hide a pregnancy. In retrospect, the only child I could be aborting was Carlos's baby, I never thought about it then, but I am glad that monster's baby left my body. Interestingly, no one ever thought, I could have been pregnant by him.

That diagnosis became a green light to an escalation of abuse that created a living hell. I remember my mouth watering, having an urge to throw up while my head throbbed with pain. Was it ever going to be over?

My pounding heart and the salty tears flowing down my face snapped me back to the present moment. Why couldn't they leave me alone and allow me to have a life.

Would I ever repay the debt of them taking me into their home? Hadn't I given them enough already? I prayed that I was just imagining seeing their car. That fear was getting the best of me. But as I got closer to the middle of the block, I recognized their white oversized Cadillac.

Our eyes locked and I could feel the venom in Lucy's eyes. I could see her lips moving but the voices and scenes in my head were so loud, I could not hear her. I walked faster and faster, pretending I was in one of those frequent repetitive dreams when I would find myself flying. And then I noticed them, Papito in the driver's seat and Lucy laughing. I started running. This was not the first time they had come around my job and started a scandal. The last time, they called me derogatory names and threatened to kick the shit out of me, names such as Hija de la gran puta, mala agradecida, which translated means ungrateful and daughter of a great bitch, this was one of their favorite sayings.

It seemed like they might have been trying to get me fired, shame me or scare me into quitting. I thought maybe they were trying to force me into returning to their home. I would never return. There was no amount of fear that would make me voluntarily get in the car with them. I ran and ran, stumbling down the stairs to the train station, afraid to look back, holding my train token so tightly that I forgot I was holding it. And just as I went through the turnstile, the Queens #7 train pulled in.

It was not until I was home in my room that I realized I had wet my pants. My body was shaking and the tears would not stop. It felt like forever before I calmed down and the pain in my heart eased. It took several hours to quiet the thoughts and begin to feel safe. I did not know if my body would ever stop shaking. They nearly gave me a heart attack but I did not give in, fall apart, or run back to them. I refused to ask them for forgiveness and beg them not to hurt me. I was safe in my furnished room in the rooming house. I would be safe until tomorrow was what I told myself as I nodded off to sleep.

The rooming house was such a blessing. While I was alone in my room, I also had company. That gave me a sense of safety. It felt good to be among independent, responsible adult women. At times, I could not believe I was holding my own. I had a job, a place to live and was managing fine. Every week, I collected my envelope with my week's pay in cash.

Using a series of envelopes, I would put aside money for my travel to and from work, for food, rent, cigarettes and snacks. Occasionally I had a little bit of change left which went in my yellow plastic piggy bank. I needed nothing else.

Living on my own was an okay experience. There were times I felt lonely and scared. To go from living with a large family to living on my own was a drastic change. My father and mother had disappointed me. I was disconnected from my siblings, Luis, Antonio, Daniel and Zulema. I did not know where they were or how to reach them and was scared to death of running into Lucy and Carlos. But my sense of relief was much greater than the loneliness and fear I felt being on my own.

The rooming house gave me more than just safety, I had a sense of being a free-at-last adult. The women were kind and generous. Some of them treated me like their little sister. They were impressed with my maturity and autonomy. I am sure they were curious about me but they did not poke around. They respected my privacy.

One woman—Veronica—turned out to be the exception to the privacy rule. Intrigued by the fact that I seldom left the house, she exhibited concern about my limited social interactions. Whenever she saw me leaving the house, she inquired if I was going on an errand. She would also wonder whether I was going to visit my parents. Mostly I just said no and provided no follow up information. I knew she probably thought I was odd. I smiled and let her think as she wished.

Veronica shared things about herself and her family back in Columbia. I gathered that loneliness was an issue for her too. Her activities seemed to be limited to working and going to night school where she studied English as a Second Language. In fact, learning to speak English was the interest that connected the two of us. Veronica found it fascinating that I spoke proper Spanish and spoke English as well. Occasionally, she asked me for help with her assignments. Sometimes she just wanted to have a simple conversation in English. Her teacher had encouraged her to practice speaking the language. I did not mind helping her. It made me feel useful. Truth be told, it also helped me feel less alone.

As time went on, Veronica and I became more like friends. Gradually, I began to tell her about my family. I explained how my father had taught me to read and write in Spanish and encouraged me to read El Diario La Prenza (The Daily Press) and how I would spend time with him and his blackboard. I did not care that she knew that I missed my dad, that I had not seen him for a long time and did not even know where he lived. I could tell when she felt uncomfortable with the conversation because she would suddenly ask if I wanted tea and off to the kitchen she ran. If she thought my not being in contact with my parents was strange, I wondered what she would think if she knew about Lucy and Carlos? I never shared any of that with her and I simply let her do most of the talking.

Veronica had dreams of visiting her family in Colombia. She spoke about her sisters and mother and how much she missed them. She would tell me about how beautiful her country was, the mountains and beautiful blue-green-water beaches.

She spoke of the food, music, and the open and friendly people. But she lived happily in Jackson Heights, Queens. "Queens is like a little South America," she would say. And off she would go into another story about her people and the country where she was born.

9

My First Love

Around the time Veronica completed her ESL class, she invited me to a party. She had worked hard and felt proud of the progress she had made in learning English. She could hold brief conversations and knew how to ask and how to respond to questions pertaining to name, age, home address, birth country and the like. She knew numbers, colors, names of some foods, like rice, beans, chicken, banana, and apples—and could name a few animals and translate a few words. This was a good start but Veronica needed many more ESL classes before English would become her second language.

"We're having a potluck party for our graduating class at La Guardia Community College in Queens. I would love it if you would come with me. There will be lots of great food, international food. You will get to meet my classmates and teachers. It should be a lot of fun. I want you to meet Cesar, a young Ecuadorian guy who's always asking me to introduce someone to him." Veronica said with a chuckle.

It had been a long time since I had been to a party. The idea sounded interesting but a bit daunting. I worried I would feel out of place and awkward. People always wanted to know where I lived, where I was from, if I had a family and where they were. They also wanted to know why a sixteen-year-old was living in a rooming house? I never knew how to respond to these questions. People sometimes asked if I was attending school and were surprised when I told them I was not.

Maybe I should go to the party and meet Veronica's Ecuadorian friend. I did not even know what it meant to meet someone. Did that mean like hooking me up? I told her I would think about it. Really, what I meant was that I would think about how to get out of it.

Not only had it been a while since I had been to a party other than at the Institute, but it had also been a while since I had been to a school. I could—and did—often brag about knowing English and Spanish and how I went to secretarial school. But deep inside, I always felt ashamed that I had dropped out of High School. My formal education had ended when I left Lucy's house and went to the Dominican Republic with my father. A year later when I returned to her house, high school was out of the question. I was grateful that they had at least sent me to a trade school, The Spanish American Institute in New York, where I learned secretarial skills.

Veronica did not give up and for the next few days she kept mentioning the party.

"It'll be a lot of fun. You never go anywhere or do anything. Don't tell me you can't come. I know you don't have anything else to do," she said.

A couple of days before the party, she told me that the teacher asked them to feel free to invite their family.

Since her classmates would bring their spouses, partners or family members and she had no one she could bring, she stressed how much it would mean to her if I would come.

I was surprised that she felt that way about me. She had always shown me kindness and care. We had friendly conversations. I knew she liked me.

She had been trying to get to know me ever since I moved in. On the other hand, I had been the one to keep distance between us. I was afraid of being viewed as a good for-nothing person with a dark history and no family to speak of. And so, I decided to go.

Veronica was so excited. Her descriptions of what to expect turned out to be right on. From Colombia, El Salvador, Honduras, Ecuador, and the Dominican Republic—a spread of delicious dishes covered the table and then some. Intense smells and amazing colors and textures of the foods appealed to all my senses.

For instance, I never realized there were so many ways to make potato salad. Some had veggies in them and others had fruit. Another seemed more like a complete dish, potatoes, eggs, veggies, cod fish and lots of onions, my favorite. Later I would discover that the sister of the Ecuadorian guy had brought it. I tried foods I had never even heard of before. Pupusas from El Salvador. Ceviche from Colombia with some nice jumbo shrimps. The tamales from Honduras were one of my favorites along with the roast pork brought by a Dominican woman. All of that, along with some arroz con gandules brought by a Puerto Rican guy, kept me quite busy.

Veronica wanted me to meet her friends.

Introductions started with, "This is Maria, who comes from.... This is Pedro from…"

I enjoyed meeting people, but as the night wore on there seemed to be a lot of confusion. The music, loud talking, the eating and all the broken English with many different accents amounted to more stimulation than I had been exposed to in an exceptionally long time. Every country seemed to have a vastly different accent or dialect. For example, I was used to talking to Dominicans, Puerto Ricans, and Cubans. But the accent of the South and Central Americans was vastly different. This one guy came up to me, supposedly speaking English and when I did not understand him, he spoke louder. Why did he think speaking louder would make his language clearer?

And then Veronica came toward me with a man. The moment I saw him my heart skipped a beat.

"This is my friend Cesar."

He was kind of cute—black wavy hair, medium built, sweet dimples, and a kind smile. Cesar immediately extended his hand and introduced himself.

"My name is Santa," I said, pretending to be confident.

Since leaving Lucy's house, I had adopted a way of presenting confidently and securely within myself. Even when fear arose, I got good at not allowing myself to feel it. Deep inside I felt that if I could survive that house, I could survive anything. So, when I felt a void in the pit of my stomach—the way you feel when you are at the very top of a roller coaster just about to head down—I would close my eyes and let go. I knew that the feeling did not mean I couldn't handle it but that I was about to handle it.

"How long have you been coming to the class?" I asked, and added, "Have you enjoyed it?"

"Yeah, I've learned a lot and I'm looking forward to continuing to learn more. I need a teacher like you "Necesito una maestra como tu." he said in Spanish, wanting to be able to speak English the way I did.

"I don't know about being your teacher but I can certainly help. Like a tutor if you really need help."

I had no idea where that came from. In the year that my father left me in the DR, I worked at a school for a little while teaching ESL. I could tutor Cesar, but what I really wanted to know is, was he hitting on me? Any man who offered kindness, compliments, or attention, certainly was hitting on me and just wanted to use me. How does one distinguish this kind of stuff anyway? I did not want to seem conceited and pretentious nor did I want to assume something that was not true.

When he asked, "Where are you from and where do you live?" I casually explained that Veronica and I lived in the same rooming house, that I was born in the Dominican Republic but was raised in New York City.

He seemed cool. The more I checked him out the more handsome he looked, though I did notice that his Levi jeans were so long that the hems were folded up more than just a few inches. He wore a long sleeve dress shirt and sneakers. He looked mixed-matched, what I would call country. But I said to myself, girl, hem those pants and take him shopping and he will be fine. Who was I to talk?

At that moment, I felt empowered and strong. It was as if I was standing there—hair in a huge floppy afro, wearing my favorite bell-bottom jeans with suspenders, platform shoes, my hands on my hips—saying, "aren't I bad!" I did not know what it was about the outfit but whatever it was, it fit right in with my don't-mess-with-me attitude.

Although neither of us seemed to fit in with the class crowd, Cesar and I were clearly from two different worlds.

I sensed his nervousness and awkwardness. He spoke too fast and seldom stopped to get responses or to listen. His talk was all about experiences in Ecuador, naming different areas and names of people as though they lived just down the street, folks that everyone knew.

I thought it might be nice to have a boyfriend, a real one. I wondered if he might have been thinking about me like that. Then I caught myself and decided such a thought needed to go right out of my mind.

Looking back, I wish I had asked him about his first impressions of me. I could not afford to make anything up or to be wrong about what might turn out to be an innocent gesture toward making a new friend. Although periodically Cesar checked in with his sister, he did return to where I stood with Veronica and hung around us most of the time.

During one of those return times, I heard myself saying, "I'm going to the cafeteria to get a drink".

Immediately, Cesar said, "Oh, I'll come with you."

I liked Cesar but I had had too many experiences with being told what I needed, wanted, or should do. Never again would I allow anyone to boss me around. I caught myself getting too far ahead again. The guy asked me to consider tutoring him. He did not ask to be my boyfriend. I didn't even know if he liked me that way or if I liked him that way. All of this was going through my head as he and I walked to the cafeteria.

Once we got there, I asked him, "Do you want something to drink?"

I walked toward the coin-operated juice and soda machine. Surprised, he gestured as if to say something but before he could open his mouth, I was at it again.

"Well, do you want something? I can handle it, I said with an attitude. Or are you one of those guys who doesn't think women should and can pay for them?"

I saw the shock on his face. His expression seemed to ask, "What's up with this chick?"

I thought about launching into a lecture about women's roles or something totally unnecessary at that moment. I also thought about making a comment indicating my lack of interest in him and my being okay with him not being interested in me. The idea that he might be attracted to me made me so uncomfortable that I'd rather pretend or convince myself that there was absolutely no attraction. That would make everything simple and clear. The uncertainty was uncomfortable as was the confusion that the physical attraction brought up. I bought the drinks, went back to the party, and sat down.

I was so wired up. Cesar had done nothing to me, yet I felt annoyed, angry, and defensive. Little did I know that there would be many future experiences filled with unexplainable anger and defensiveness.

One day I would understand that what I was going through was the long-term effects of the sexual, emotional and psychological trauma I had lived through. My defensiveness would often show up as me being over serious. I would also discover my difficulty in separating humor from fact and how easily it was for me to be offended.

I remember Cesar saying, "Niña, calmate, cojelo suave, tota bien," in his improper Spanish. In English he was saying, Girl, calm down. Take it easy. Everything is good. Then he chuckled as if to say, "Really, it isn't that serious."

I had no idea that Cesar had recently arrived at the US illegally and knew no English. He could barely read and write his own ethnic language, Spanish.

I began to help him with his English. I would fire off instructions.

"Make index cards to study with. Put the word in Spanish on one side and the English word and a sentence on the other side. Whenever and wherever, you must read your cards. Watch English-speaking television programs and read the paper in English instead of Spanish. You must practice all the time and you cannot be embarrassed. Speak in English even if you don't know what the hell you're saying."

We would crack up laughing because sometimes, that was exactly what he would do. We could be sitting on the stoop outside the house and he would just break out speaking in English. He would string a bunch of words he knew into one sentence and then say you know what I mean which sounded like, *yew no wha I meen,* in his very broken English. He was so good at saying hysterical things with a straight face. He was always telling jokes and making me laugh. In retrospect, I think this was his way of dealing with his inadequacies.

I found it easy and fun to spend time with Cesar. He liked being silly and expected me to be silly with him. For him, being in the US was such a big deal. It was like a dream come true–finally in the country of opportunities. Going places, seeing what there was to see in the city, delighted him. This was how he came up with the idea that we could take our classes on the road.

"Let's go to the park. You can show me some of the words that relate to being there. We can bring lunch and hang out. You bring the sandwiches since you're the woman." He teased.

I did. I made peanut butter sandwiches, threw in a couple of apples and bottles of water and off to Central Park we went.

I hadn't been to Central Park since I was a kid. We went on the merry-go-round, climbed a few mountains, and stopped in at the zoo. We practiced English but really, we just hung out.

We would go to Central Park often. Usually, I brought our lunch or snacks from home but one day I emptied a whole $18.00 from my piggy bank and went all out.

I called myself taking Cesar out on an official date. For some reason, although I insisted on being independent and unconventional, we agreed that the next time we went out, he would pay. Cesar showed up Saturday afternoon as we had agreed. I was ready when he rang the doorbell.

When I opened the door the scent of his cologne rushed in. Cesar wore his same rolled up jeans and white tee shirt. His sunglasses and a big red headscarf stuck in his back pocket. He looked cool, fresh, and unencumbered.

"Mira Santa," he said as he excitedly held up his newest discovery. Roller blades had just hit the streets and everyone was either rollerblading or learning how to.

"Do you know how to ride those?" I asked"

"No but I'm about to learn." He answered.

"You're going to fall on your face and break your pretty sunglasses," I laughed.

As soon as we entered the park on 86th street, Cesar put on his roller blades.

"Push me," he said.

Off he went.

My job soon became to help him up and off the ground and push him off again when he got back up and found his balance. He was determined to learn how to roller blade and he did. But only after he fell many times and got a few scrapes.

"I think I'm getting a bit hungry. This scraping you off the ground and from between lamp poles is hard work," I mumbled, containing my laughter.

"You're next. Don't think you're going to get out of this." He said sternly with a smile.

We had built up an appetite so we walked up to the first hotdog truck vendor we saw. The smell of hotdogs and pretzels made my mouth water. Cesar was used to the "perro calientes" hotdogs but the numerous condiments were new to him.

"Hey, it's my treat. What do you want?" I asked.

Intrigued by the whole set up, he ended up getting two hotdogs with the works, a knish with mustard—as per my suggestion—and a coke. I wanted two dogs but did not want to seem un-lady-like by eating too much.

Besides, I wanted to save room for a pretzel with mustard, I loved the salt on the pretzels, a Knish, and an ice cream cone. The day was still young, so I got a hotdog with mustard and piping hot onions.

We found a spot on the ground not far from the hotdog vendor and sat down to eat. Cesar made a mess of himself. He had way too much stuff on his hotdog—onions, cabbage, mustard, and ketchup, were dripping all over the place.

I found it endearing, and truth be told, to my surprise, I was getting awfully warm and sexually aroused. The way he ate his hotdog, trying to catch the drippings while licking his fingers and lips. I figured all bets were off, no need to impress.

As I took my last bite, we went back to the vendor and got my knish. We sat around for a while and just people watched and talked. It was such a fun day in the park. Cesar just loved telling me stories about being back home in Ecuador and about his mother, whom he loved dearly.

Cesar had come from a poor working-class family. He was the eldest male of the six siblings. There were four sisters and a younger brother, who came to the states with him. When Cesar was twelve his father died and he took pride in taking care of his family since then. I could understand why he was so glad to be in the US. He spoke about it as the country of opportunities. I shared with him that I too came from a large family but unfortunately was not in contact with them. I appreciated him for not asking questions. I hoped that the day would come when I could share my stories with him.

We were like two kids. He was new to the states and I was new to a life without violence and fear. He got to introduce me to the Ecuadorian ways and I got to show him around. My excellent English skills allowed us to explore places and things that otherwise he would not have been able to explore at that time.

Cesar was always asking me to translate.

"What does that mean? How do you say that?"

I read and translated street signs, advertisements on buses and trains. I respected his determination to learn English and was impressed with how quickly he picked it up. He practiced speaking with anyone and everyone he could, without shyness or embarrassment.

One Sunday afternoon when he came to pick me up, he was all dressed up. This was a date he had planned all on his own. I am sure he asked his sister for suggestions. When I opened the door, he looked good. I was impressed.

Days before our date he told me, "Dress nice. Maybe wear a dress. We are going to a nice place."

Very rarely did I wear dresses. I felt safer in jeans and sneakers. I would not risk being blamed for being promiscuous and most importantly if I had to run I could.

I was excited. My first official adult date. I had to challenge myself to show up like a lady wanting to be attractive for her boyfriend. Yet, the loud voices in my head just kept warning me.

When I saw him, I had the sense that things were going to move to another level and perhaps this was what I wanted. Cesar wore black slacks and a baby blue shirt. I could tell he had just shaved and gotten a haircut. He smelled incredible. I wore a white dress and was very mindful to not wear heels. I did not want to look taller than he was.

This was the first time that I invited him in. I told him I needed a few moments and asked him to wait in the living room. I ran to the bedroom, sprayed on some perfume, and put on lipstick. When I returned, he stood up and looked at me.

"You look beautiful."

Before I realized it, we were face to face. He kissed me on the lips. Our very first kiss.

"You ready?" he asked.

10

Lessons in Love

Boy, was I ready? I was so excited. My very first boyfriend. I had a boyfriend when I was twelve and lived with my mother. His name was Jesus. Occasionally we kissed, held hands, and watched television. But this was the real thing. Cesar and I were both adults. And just as quickly as I had felt the excitement from our kiss came the anxiety and nervousness. Cesar must have noticed because he gently eased away from me.

"Come on, let's go." He said taking my hand.

Clearly this restaurant was not his choice. It was French and quite nice but foreign to both of us. Cesar looked like a little child, all proud and in awe. His chest could not have been any more puffed up. The greeter brought us to our table, pulled my seat out for me and then for Cesar. Then he laid our napkins on our lap. I had been to a fancy restaurant like this before but had not ever had my napkin laid on my lap. The greeter proceeded to place open menus in front of us and indicated that our waiter would be there momentarily.

"This is really a nice place. Can you handle this?" I asked.

Immediately he said, "Yes, you'll have to help me with the menu." Cesar said.

By then our waiter had come around to take our drink orders and tell us what the specials were. I barely understood what the waiter was saying. He was not speaking English. All I said when he was done was thank you and bring us two cokes. As he walked away, Cesar and I just looked at each other. We were both tickled. What on earth were we doing here?

"Are you ready to go in the kitchen and do dishes or something?" I said as we broke out laughing.

We had a wonderful time. Once we realized that the prices on the menu were a bit steep, we agreed to order appetizers and desserts only. This was my first-time having escargot and Cesar's first-time having liver pate. Between that and the bread and butter, we were set. When we finally got the bill, we were relieved. We had made it out safely this time. No dish washing for us.

Cesar and I had many more dates, sometimes to Central Park, others to the park in Corona, Queens. We went to the movies and out to eat, always referring to that first date. We reminisced about that day often and laughed about it for years.

The day came when Cesar invited me to his sister's house. He wanted me to meet the rest of his family, particularly his brother. I had met his sister at the school party but it had been a brief introduction. His sister Gladys lived with her husband, Cesar, and his brother in Woodside, in Queens, New York.

When we got to Cesar's home, I was surprised that Gladys was not home. She was at work and was not expected for a while. He invited me to sit and asked if I wanted something to drink. Reluctantly, I accepted. He then invited me to go upstairs to, "see his room."

The moment I walked into the house and heard that no one else was home, I knew something was up. Going up to his room confirmed it. I assumed we would be making out. I was not ready for what followed. Cesar gently reassured me that no one would be home for a while. Before I knew it, our making out transitioned to making love. I felt a barrage of mixed emotions. This experience reminded me of when I was a kid back home. I did want to share that intimate moment with Cesar and was excited about him wanting me in that way. But I also felt like it might be too soon for us to take our relationship to that level. I felt too that it was not appropriate to be intimate at his sister's home and in her bed. It turned out that Cesar did not have a room to show me after all.

But what was bizarre were my tears. When we finished making love I began to cry. Cesar asked me what was wrong and if he had hurt me. I assured him that he was very tender and that it was pleasurable. But something had saddened me deeply. In my experience with Cesar, I could see why they refer to sexual intercourse as making love. I had been part of many sexual events but never associated them with love. This felt special, different. But why was I crying? Why was I comparing this to those horrible times at Lucy's house? My runaway feelings and thoughts were not intentional. I did not want to be thinking about my past but I could not stop my mind from going there.

That night I had difficulty falling asleep. When I did fall asleep, I had horrific dreams. The memories of the many times Carlos had forced me to be sexual with him would not cease.

It was a few weeks after returning from DR and living at their home that the waking nightmares began. Carlos concluded that I was being sexual outside of the home and therefore should have no choice but to be sexual with him. Whether I wanted to or not, no was not an option. Lucy's response? Instead of being angry with him, she had directed her anger at me. She was not going to let me destroy her family again. This time, if I wanted her man, I needed to go through her. What that meant was, I was going to need to "do" her as well. There was no more pretending Carlos was in love with me or I with him. There were no promises of a fantasy tomorrow.

Every day, living at Carlos and Lucy's house, was worse. The fights, the beatings, the forced drug use, it all escalated. Heavy into voyeurism, Carlos got off on orchestrating and watching the many disgusting scenes he forced on Lucy and me. He got a kick at watching me anally penetrate Lucy with a dildo, this was after me being sodomized by him. The impact of those experiences haunted me as I tried to have my first normal sexual experience.

How could I explain to Cesar the thoughts that ensued after our first love-making encounter?

How could I face the shame, embarrassment, and the fear of blame and judgment? How could something so sweet, gentle, and beautiful be associated with the nightmare of my childhood? Would it ever be over? Would I ever be able to put it behind me?

A few months after our encounter, Cesar and I began to discuss moving in together. Given the fact that I lived in a rooming house and he lived in his sister's house, we thought it was logical to find a place together. We found a furnished basement apartment just a few blocks away from my rooming house. It was perfect for us. Inexpensive with plenty of space.

Cesar and his brother came to the rooming house to help me move my things. Over time I had accumulated a few kitchen things, clothes, etc. I did not have much but it was a start. I had lots of experience with shopping carts. In only a couple of trips, I was all moved in. Pushing our shopping cart down the streets of Jackson Heights fit right in with the neighborhood culture.

Cesar had even less stuff. His clothes, a few pieces of exercise equipment and his roller blades.

"My sister said she's going to put some things together for us. She said she has some extra kitchen stuff and some sheets and towels. Would that be okay?" He asked.

"I think we should take everything but punches," I said, and we laughed.

About a year after moving in together, Cesar and I decided to get married. We loved each other and seemed to get along. Cesar needed to marry to become a US resident. So why not marry? The sooner the better.

Cesar wore a black suit to the event of our nuptials. I had my hair done by the neighborhood Dominican hair dressers and wore a knee-high white sleeveless dress and black jacket. I pinned red roses to the lapels of our jackets. Cesar and I agreed we did not want anything fancier.

"I don't need for us to have a fancy ceremony. I just ask that we take real (professional) pictures at a studio." I told Cesar who happily agreed.

Our witnesses were Cesar's sister and her husband who met us downtown at City Hall. We were married in New York City on a weekday. The entire ceremony took all of fifteen minutes.

As we were leaving the building, a man handed me a bouquet of flowers and asked, "Would you like a picture?"

Cesar and I posed for our first picture as Mr. And Mrs. Jimenez.

Excited and sad simultaneously, I found nothing special about this "should-be-special," day.

For some reason, I did not feel I had the right to make any demands on my new husband. Neither one of us could afford much more than what we had done.

I told myself that what mattered was our love for each other. I was happy to be able to say that I was now a Jimenez. No longer did I have to be associated with the Molina's and their legacy of abuse and violence. I could finally start my own family.

Cesar summoned me out of my reflection. "Santa, Santa, where are you? Are you okay? Gladys has been asking you if you want to go to McDonald's for lunch."

I had been so deep in thought I had not heard him at first.

"Sure, that would be nice."

A couple of weeks later, after we had saved up enough money, we got back into our wedding outfits and stopped by the local photo studio for our wedding pictures. I was happy we were following up on our agreement. Our photographs were pretty and I was proud of them. Cesar and I made a cute couple. We had several duplicates made, small wallet sizes, and a large one that I got framed and put up in our living room.

Soon after, we filed for Cesar's green card. Cesar and Gladys suggested that I file for Naturalization before I submitted an immigration petition for Cesar. Something about me being a US Citizen helping to expedite his immigration petition once we filed it. Immigration investigated and later interviewed me. I was amazed by all the information they had on me. Everything from the time I was born, the schools I had attended, places I lived, worked, who my siblings and parents were. They also knew that I had been involved with Juvenile Family Court and had been sent to an adolescent group home. They knew about me leaving the country and living in the Dominican Republic for almost a year. I waited for them to bring up the things I had experienced at Lucy's house but that never came up.

Within a year or two, Cesar was on his way to becoming naturalized. Cesar and his sister were right, me being a US Citizen expedited the process. Cesar was not just legal in the US; he was a naturalized American.

Living in Jackson Heights, Queens was like being in a Latin American country. On a Friday afternoon, I saw people walking up and down the streets. Stores lined the streets and there was music on loudspeakers announcing their weekly specials. Children screamed and begged parents for this, that and the other. Men eyed the women who walked by and commented on their butt, breast, or anything,

Most of the stores had their merchandise spilling out onto the sidewalk. People were doing their shopping before they entered the store. There were also street vendors. They did well competing with the stores. Folks were selling just about everything from food to clothes and at times even furniture out of trucks.

Walking up and down Junction Boulevard or Roosevelt Avenue could be entertaining if you were looking to be entertained. But when you're just trying to get things done, it could be distracting and at times irritating.

People were so distracted that they bumped into each other like bumper cars. This was the typical experience on Fridays, Saturdays, and Sundays. Imagine what it was like during holidays or summer when school was out. The people in my neighborhood had recreated the communities they came from and where they felt the safest. This was the part of the Dominican Republic my mother talked about all the time. This is what she missed living in midtown Manhattan. She probably would've been much happier in Jackson Heights.

During Holy Week on that typical, yet auspicious Good Friday, the Jackson Heights buzz was at its peak. The traditional Catholic ritual of abstaining from eating red meat on Good Friday had sent me in search of fresh fish. I set out to get my fish and return home. The moment I hit the intersection of Roosevelt Avenue and Junction Blvd it was on.

"Stay focused and just get what you came out for," I told myself. If I could make it to Roosevelt Avenue and out of the fish market with nothing but the fish, I would have been successful. Before long, I was approached by the lady who sold the tamales.

"Tamales de pescado," (fish tamales) she said.

I had tried the pork tamales but I wondered what fish tamales would be like.

"What the hell," I said to myself and decided to buy a couple.

Just as I prepared to pay the tamales lady, the guy selling churros came by. I had seen him punching his cart as I walked down the street and had resisted stopping. It was almost as if he knew I would be an easy sell.

"Churros, caliente."

I knew they were hot and sweet and I could taste the powdered sugar on them. I imagined they were nice and crunchy as well.

Okay, so I did fall for the excitement. I knew I had better get to the fish market before I ended up using my fish money.

The market was full. Everyone was preparing for Good Friday.

"Please give me four large slices of king fish," I told the salesperson. I loved seafood but had little experience buying it.

We rarely had anything other than fish, shrimp and occasionally my father would bring home squid or shark. Sometimes we would get seafood at the Chinese restaurant with our fried rice or vegetable dishes.

As I dashed out of the store to make my way back to the house the sight of a woman just outside the market door stopped me in my tracks.

She looked familiar. I seemed familiar to her as well. She not only seemed familiar, but she also felt familiar. In a flash, I knew it was my sister Zulema.

I had not seen her since my mother, Antonio and I left our home on 84th Street about 4 years ago.

"Lema? Is that you?"

Before she could answer, we embraced and were in tears.

"How are you? What are you doing here? Are you okay? Do you live around here? Who do you live with?" She asked, all while she was holding me in a warm embrace.

We looked at each other in disbelief. She told me she lived right up the street with her boyfriend Narciso.

"Remember Narciso?"

For a moment, time stopped and we were the only two on Roosevelt Avenue.

"Permiso, permiso." I heard a woman say.

We were blocking the doorway to the fish market.

"Come in and wait for me," Zulema told me.

It was magical to have found my sister on a Good Friday. I felt like God was looking out for me. I had been disconnected from my family for a long time. Primarily it was because of fear and paranoia. After leaving Lucy's home, I never tried to contact anyone in my family. Safety was the greatest priority. Running into my sister Zulema was such a gift.

I did not want to leave her side and it was clear that she did not want to leave mine. That day, she invited me over to her house. She lived in an apartment with her boyfriend who became the father of her two sons. He was not home from work yet, for which we were both glad. This allowed us time to catch up.

Lema, as I grew to refer to her, reminded me so much of my mother. She was a bit old fashioned.

She immediately invited me to the kitchen.

"Can I offer you un cafecito," (a small coffee) she asked.

I had never had Espresso. Children drank their coffee with milk or better yet, their milk with coffee. I had not yet graduated to the adult version which was a strong, black, and sweet coffee.

"Of course," I said gratefully.

She explained that she needed to start dinner for Narciso. While she cooked, we talked about our lives. She shared with me how she came to live in Jackson Heights. She said her relationship with Narciso was okay.

"He's a good man. He works hard. With me working full time at my job in the Bronx, we do okay. But "no hay felicidad completa" (there is no complete happiness).

He really would rather not have children. He already has children. As a matter of fact, he has a daughter my age. He feels like he is too old to have more."

"Things change, Lema. You never know what the future holds. Look at us. Who would have thought we would ever run into each other," I said?

I opened up and shared my Lucy story with her. To my surprise, she had her own Lucy and Carlos horror story. Throughout the years, Lucy had built a lot of resentment towards Lema. There had been something about feeling like Lema had chosen Narciso and her relationship with him over her relationship with Lucy. Lema shared about the many times Lucy showed up at her previous place of residence and created scandals. It saddened me to hear that Lucy had made Lema's life miserable as well. We agreed that we would protect ourselves from her. Like me, Lema had distanced herself from the rest of the family for the same reason.

Lema's apartment really took me back to our past. As I sat there keeping her company and chatting with her, I broke out laughing.

"Lema, I can't believe that you have plastic over your tablecloth, just like mom did."

Lema lived in a row apartment just like the one we grew up in. She did not only have a plastic protective cover on her kitchen table, but she also put them over her living room furniture. And the many knick knacks that were oh so classic.

Lema had a proposal for me. "Hey, how would you like to work at the place where I work? They are hiring account representatives. It is a good company and they give great bonuses at the end of the year. They also offer medical benefits and vacation leave. I'm sure with your secretarial and typing skills and my recommendation, you'll be hired on the spot."

She went on to share her enthusiasm about us going to and from work together and how we would have lots of time to catch up.

"I can't believe that my "la Cucuta" is all grown up." Lema said affectionately.

"It would be nice to spend time together. I will work on my resume and you can check in with your boss. But you must promise not to ever call me Cucuta in public."

We laughed and talked about how happy we were to have found each other. The truth was I would have loved to work somewhere else. I was still worried about Lucy and Carlos showing up at my job. The place where I worked reminded me of the abuse and embarrassment I suffered. I was ready to put those experiences behind me.

In the meantime, Lema and I got to spend a lot of time together. I visited her apartment often and got reacquainted with Narciso. He was a cool guy. Very proper, kind, and generous. We reminisced about the times at our Manhattan apartment.

He reminded me of the times when my mother would insist that they take me with them on their outings. He mentioned how I was often sent out with him and Lema to the movies and joked about how glad he was that I liked movies.

"Well, I also liked raisinets and popcorn," I said, and we laughed.

It was nice to spend time with Lema without Narcisco. We had so much to talk about. Eventually, I ended up being hired at her place of work. The work was different than I was used to and it felt good to be able to learn it. Instead of doing reception work, I got to take customer orders, prepare paperwork, and follow up on orders all the way to production. I also got to interface with the customers and keep them updated. The company Lema and I worked at manufactured elevators and elevator parts. It was nice seeing the name of our products on elevators in public buildings.

I got rather good at my job and soon the Molina sisters were known as a dynamic duo. I enjoyed working at a big company and making Lema proud was a bonus. We rode the #6 train for two and a half hours every day to and from work. I told her about Cesar and how much I liked him.

For Cesar and me, the basement apartment became an oasis. From Friday to Sunday, we would hang out together. I cooked a feast and we would eat, drink beer, wine or have a few shots of Aguardiente. Then we would listen to music and dance around the apartment. We laughed about the silliest things, particularly about Cesar's dancing.

"I don't know what they dance in Ecuador," I would say to him. Cesar claimed it was the Cumbia. I found out later from his sister that Cesar was doing his own version of Cumbia. The truth was he could not dance. I, on the other hand, was an expert at merengue and salsa. I taught him how to dance.

"Dancing merengue is a little like marching in place with an attitude. Keep your head up, your arms relaxed, keep your arms at the chest level and your hips soft." This is how my dad showed me to dance.

Cesar would try. "It's too much to remember. Let's just dance."

I would discover that in dancing, as in other areas of his life, Cesar was good for creating his own moves and even following his own beat. And that was good because he was not able to follow the beat of the music.

"Control your hips. The men just slightly move their hips. The women are the ones that get into the swinging of their hips and waist," I'd remind him.

Cesar always ranted about how the woman's part was more fun. That is when he would break into his own thing,

"Wait, I need a break. I promise I'll follow in a moment."

His brother and I would fall out laughing and cheer him on. Eventually, over the years, he became a rather good dancer.

Cesar was affectionate, generous with his time and helpful around the house. Cooking for us became one of his favorite things, especially cooking traditional Ecuadorian foods. That was until he learned how to make a few Italian dishes. Then he thought he was an expert at making Stromboli, pizza, and lasagna, I did wonder where he learned to make these dishes. Cesar's brother often joined us. It was fascinating to hear them talk about their experiences in Ecuador. I admired their close relationship. They were like real friends.

Over time, the number of parties, feasts, the alcohol consumption, and pot smoking kept increasing. Once Cesar got started drinking, he could not stop. Often, he would drink himself sick. I got good at cleaning him and his mess up and getting him into bed. I was dedicated to being a good wife and taking care of him. I believed that he would stop drinking someday for me because he loved me. It was the same thing I had believed about my father.

On Friday nights, the drinking would start and continue throughout the entire weekend. In truth, we all drank—Cesar, his brother and me. But Cesar was the only one who got stupid drunk. He would drink until he would black out. I was somewhat relieved, even grateful, that unlike my father who would get violent, Cesar simply blacked out and went to sleep. On several occasions, he came home from work on Fridays, already drunk.

He would tell me, "The guys invited me for a beer. I really didn't mean to stay out drinking again."

On one of those Fridays, he came home with his hand bandaged up. He was working as a carpenter at a factory and went out drinking at lunch. He had sawed off his index finger with an electric saw. I did not know whether to be angry or sorry. Not only was Cesar hurt, but he was also drunk and jobless again.

But what Cesar and I shared was mostly magic, fun and beauty. We were known as the ideal couple; we did most things together. He enjoyed biking, running, and playing soccer; as well as going to the movies, restaurants, bars, and nightclubs. We made frequent visits to his sister's and my sister Lema's apartment. We were always hanging out at the park or taking on a biking trail.

Cesar was determined to run the New York City Marathon and that he did, several times.

"Are you coming today? This is going to be a long one," he would ask.

"How long? And you better tell me the truth. The last time we went out you almost killed me."

He would laugh and tell me, "Stop being a baby. All you have to do is make sure I don't get too thirsty, feed me, rub me down and give me mouth to mouth resuscitation when I need it."

"I think you got the easy part of this deal, buddy. I get to be your caddy girl, masseur, nurse, cook and you expect me to kiss your sweaty, stinky self? I may need to take up running." I'd say.

He'd slap my butt and say, "Oh come on, you love taking care of me. You'd do anything to come along."

We would break out laughing and start chasing each other around the apartment, laughing and screaming.

Often on the weekends, I would join him for his training runs. We would pack our backpack and spend hours out on the road. Cesar ran and I biked, walked and at times took the train and met him down the road. I swear, sometimes I felt like he was trying to kill me.

What an inspiration he was. He had set his mind to get all that he came to the US of America to get. He worked hard to learn English and continued to take classes at LaGuardia Community College. Seemingly out of the blue one day, he came home all excited.

"We should get our GED's. We need to go to la Universidad (the University). And you know we are going. You know that, right?"

He was wired and could not stop talking about it. He had heard about an offer for free GED preparation classes at the college.

"I got you. I'll cook, clean the house, do the laundry and give you tons of licks." He said and giggled.

"You're gross. How are you going to pass that exam, Mr. Know It All?"

"We'll take it in Spanish. That way I can help you out," he answered.

I joked, "Yeah, right. That would be perfect. The blind leading the blind. You'd probably do better in English, sir."

"I'm not scared. I've got the best bilingual teacher in the whole world," he said, giving me a big hug.

A short while later, we both were studying for the GED. After a year or so, we took the exam in Spanish. With lots of help from me before the exam and a little help during the exam, we both got our GED's. Straightaway after that, we registered at LaGuardia Community College. And just as Cesar had predicted and claimed, the two of us were working on our Associates Degree from La Universidad. It was great to be back in school. College was something I never thought would happen for me. A couple of years later, I graduated from La Guardia with my associate degree.

It took Cesar three or four years but he finally got his degree too. He was right. He did have the best bilingual teacher. I enjoyed helping him.

Cesar took lots of basic preparatory courses. Many nights we stayed up studying and going over basic algebra, reading comprehension, laughing, and carrying on. I wrote many essays with him and for him. One day, I hung outside the classroom, assisting him with his writing composition exam. I did not always feel good about the cheating but we got good at it and helping him was so fulfilling to me. I was not, "una hija de puta," (a son (daughter) of a bitch) after all, I knew how to care for others. Eventually he got good at his studies. He made friends and had lots of study buddies and study groups. Getting him through college was enormous and truly a community effort. But Cesar was fulfilling his American Dream.

Cesar talked about his family all the time. How much he loved his mother. How this sister or that sister ran a home business. How his younger sister was strung out on drugs. How his uncle was like his father. How Mr. so and so was his best friend.

He would go on and on about how he wanted me to meet his mother, sisters, cousins, aunts, and people in the neighborhood.

"My mother and sisters are extremely excited about us coming to visit. They are eager to meet you. My mother asked me if you like crabs and ceviche. She wants to make sure to have the local fisherman drop off some fresh shrimp and crabs. It's been way too long since I've seen them," he said.

Other than my trip to the Dominican Republic, I had never left the US. I too was eager to meet his family. I could not wait to visit Ecuador.

"We'll need to bring a little something for them," he informed me.

"Let's make a list of everyone we need to take something to. There are too many to keep track of everyone," I told him.

I could not believe we had to bring a gift or several gifts to family, friends and even neighbors. That was a huge deal.

Cesar was returning from the country of opportunities. It was expected that he would bring gifts and be ready to treat everyone to something and of course bring cash. It seemed a little overkill to me but Cesar was not having it any other way.

A couple of months prior to our trip, the shopping would start. We spent hours at stores finding the sales. On our first trip to Ecuador, we used up all our tax refund money and maxed out our credit cards.

Arriving in Ecuador was incredible. It was like the entire neighborhood had been waiting for us. Everyone seemed to know Cesar.

"They just got here! Cesar and Santa are here!" I heard someone call out.

As we walked up to his mother's house, people just kept coming over. Before long, the house was filled with family and friends.

Ever-so-often, someone would say, "Go tell so and so that Cesar and his wife are here."

And that someone would run off.

I had never witnessed such joy and happiness at just seeing someone. They hugged Cesar and praised how good he looked. As I listened to their sentiments, I realized many of Cesar's friends and family had been doubtful he would make it back to Ecuador. He left on a work crew-ship and jumped ship in Miami, Florida.

It felt good to be surrounded by so much love. As his wife, I was automatically accepted and welcomed. You would have thought I was a queen as attentive as they were. I was asked what I wanted. They offered to get me whatever I needed. They made sure I was comfortable. They offered to cook for me and make me a drink if I wanted it. This was what a loving and happy family looked like. It was true they had issues. Issues like poverty, lack of education and drug addiction. But I could feel the love they had for each other. Being with Cesar gave me the opportunity to be part of a family and this made me feel loved as well.

We carried the suitcases with all the gifts we bought into the house and sat on the balcony. The gifting began at about two o'clock in the hot, bright sun with temperatures in the nineties. The kids laughed and ran around playing with their new electric cars, baby dolls, walkman radios, cassette players, coloring books and crayons.

Others were excited about their new outfits. New pants, dresses, tops, sneakers, and shoes. Cesar's mother was ecstatic as we discussed remodeling her kitchen, fixing the floor in the living room and purchasing a new refrigerator and stove.

Prior to coming to Ecuador, Cesar and I had discussed this. I was struck by the fact that they had been without these basic things for years.

The giveaway became a neighborhood party. There was Cumbia and salsa playing from a neighbor's turntable, food, and drinks and lots of laughter. We were at it until the night got cool and the sky was crowded with stars.

Everyday thereafter, Cesar's mother was up early preparing breakfast for Cesar and me. She was happy to serve us and eager to make us comfortable. From the minute we woke up to the minute we went to bed, we were surrounded by non-stop activity. His sisters wanted us to do hair and nails for one another. His mother was preparing lunch and dinner for the folks who were coming over. Shortly after noon Cesar would start drinking. He got drunk and sobered up at least twice every day. His mother asked him to please stop drinking in a gentle but worried motherly manner; it did not faze him a bit.

His drinking did not seem to surprise them. The night before we returned home there was a big finale party. It was terribly sad. Cesar's mother and sisters were full of sorrow that he was leaving and would not return until the next year. They cried and asked him to please take good care of himself. They ran around gathering gifts for us as send-offs. They were all incredibly grateful and wanted to show their appreciation. I still remember Cesar's mother sitting for hours picking crabs to send crab meat home with me. She knew that I loved crab meat and wanted me to have the absolute best.

These trips to Cesar's family in Ecuador became a yearly tradition. Finally, I felt like a part of a family again. I felt welcomed, respected, and honored and of course popular. Cesar and I were the talk of the neighborhood. It got to the point that when we were leaving, folks would be placing their orders to be delivered by our next visit.

Upon returning home, we would always discuss and agree that we had gone overboard. We knew we needed to be more mindful moving forward. We could not afford to continue to get in debt that way. We did the same or worse every year. We worked hard throughout the year to get out of debt only to repeat the process the following year.

Did I mind? Of course not! It felt good to share with those who clearly had so much less than I did. They were so appreciative and grateful and returned the gifts in attention, love, and care. Cesar's sisters and I became good friends. We corresponded frequently, talked often on the phone at least once a month and dreamed about a time they too would be able to come to the US.

Every year I fell more in love with Cesar. Although his drinking was a challenge, he was good hearted, generous, inspiring, and encouraging.

He was determined to get to know the US. We started with the surrounding areas by camping in Upstate New York. We soon discovered Beaver Pond Campground in the Seven Lakes area. And this became yet another tradition.

We would pack our car for the trip and a mere four hours later we were setting up our tents and building a fire. Neither one of us had ever been camping but we learned the ropes together. I was a natural, country/city girl and Cesar was a natural country guy.

We were not intimidated by the woods and doing without. We loved spending time together, playing cards, listening to music, swimming in the lake, hiking, cooking on an open fire and telling each other stories. Every year we added a few more items to our camping gear. Soon we were bringing our bikes with us. Eventually we stayed a week and invited friends to come with us.

Cesar was determined and committed to getting the most of his experience in the US. His American dream was unfolding quickly. He was going places and was taking me with him. I thanked God for his determination and our love.

Part of my being what I thought was a "good wife," entailed me being independent, not asking for or expecting Cesar to do too much. I was to be a confident and liberal wife. I could not be jealous or ask too many questions. I believed insecurity was not a good quality and that trust was essential. I wanted him to trust me and I would always trust him. I gave my husband lots of space and did not suffocate him. I later learned that what I did not want to be perceived as was co-dependent.

Cesar mainly took care of himself. I knew early in the relationship that I had to take care of myself. That included my body, mind, and spirit. And that I did or so I thought. Being independent was important yet complicated for me. I thought at first: why should anyone take care of me? I assumed taking care of myself was my own responsibility. On one hand, I thought that if I gave, I would receive. I gave to Cesar but my receiving did not come easy. I did not recognize Cesar's or other people's desire or willingness to give to me. I did not recognize it and so, it did not exist.

On the other hand, I did not expect very much. I had learned that pain and disappointment was proportional to my expectations. The fewer my expectations, the fewer the chances of my being disappointed and hurt. I was especially challenged when it came to trusting that Cesar and other people in my life had my best interest in mind.

Despite the good and happy parts of my relationship with Cesar, he would later teach me important lessons about the person I had become as a direct result of my childhood experiences.

11

My Own Reflection

Though I had no awareness of my shadows at the time, I would soon come face to face with some of the wounded parts of myself. I was extremely sensitive and was easily offended. I needed and wanted to be appreciated for my efforts and there were many. You had to show me you loved me by doing as much for me as I did for you; that was my philosophy. Anticipate my needs as I do yours. Do not criticize or overlook my efforts or accuse me of not giving my all.

There was another common scene in my relationship with Cesar; Me cooking and serving Cesar what I thought were excellent meals.

I believed I was a good cook. I enjoyed cooking large meals. After laboring to prepare meals for us, I would tell myself, "Excelente! (excellent) Another delicious meal tonight! I really put my foot in this one."

My meals always looked wonderful. They were colorful, aromatic, and tasty. Just as I had seen my mother and sisters do millions of times, I prepared the tray with plenty of food. I would be ready to receive my gifts of acknowledgement and be rewarded with the praise I desperately needed. Even though I wanted praise

I would preface serving the meal by saying, "Oh it's nothing, you don't have to thank me."

When things did not go the way I expected, it was as if a fuse were lit inside me. I would be terribly offended and I could hear myself thinking all the things I wanted to say to him.

"Is that it? I can't believe that's all you're going to eat! What's wrong with it? Is it not good enough for you?"

And I would say to him. "After all the effort I put into cooking this shit for you, you are not going to eat it. Give me the damn tray!"

With my heart pounding out of my chest, my hands shaking and the uncontrollable desire to scream, I would stomp into the kitchen.

Inside I would be thinking, after all the fucking work I had done, all he had to say was, it is a bit salty. How dare he! I had tears running down my face and the anger of an uncontrollable beast whose rage could only be tamed by exploding,

I could not throw the food in the garbage fast enough. When the food wouldn't fall out of the pot, I would say, " fuck it" and throw the whole thing out, pot and all.

He doesn't appreciate it or me anyway! Why is that I'm never appreciated? I asked myself.

I'd continued banging pots, slamming cabinets, and watching the glass shatter. Sometimes I'd just go to bed and cry myself to sleep but only after stuffing myself. That gave me a little relief but did little to address the underlying issues.

Days and sometimes weeks later, I'd remain disconnected from myself and others. This uncontrollable behavior followed me wherever life took me.

I felt trapped in myself. I fought to get out of that self-imposed prison but couldn't leave. I'd have dialogues with myself and sometimes even pleaded with myself to be released. My bad mood wouldn't change for days, sometimes weeks. Those mood swings would mostly show up at home but were not isolated to home.

Friends, family and even strangers would fall victim to my out-of-control moments. Feeling hurt, unappreciated, and victimized, I tried to handle the unbearable pain of what I viewed as rejection. My inability to reconnect kept me locked in my thoughts and trapped by my emotions. The pain was so intolerable that it would numb me, leave me speechless. Sometimes I would stop eating, to starve myself out of existence.

Banging my head on the bathroom sink, scratching myself until I drew blood, helped me to feel. It was as though I needed to punish myself for being alive, for making mistakes and disappointing others. I cannot remember all the times I threw out food, tore clothing that did not fit right, broke things that frustrated me, went off on people that did not understand me or do what I suggested. If a person did not give me what I thought I earned, or were fucking with me, it would bring out a part of me that hijacked the rest of me. I would eat until I was in pain or until diarrhea and indigestion set in as my body rejected the food. At times, I drank and smoked pot until I silenced the voices. I was already disconnected from my body and was struggling and fighting the urge to disconnect from my thoughts. I was injured and felt deeply slighted. To make sure I got what I deserved, I lashed out.

I asked myself, "I did deserve it, didn't I?"

How many times did I hear, "Can't you just let it go? Can't you not take everything so personal? Why are you so angry and sad? It is not such a big deal. You are so intense."

That is what I was often told. The fear of being hurt, rejected, or abused often led to me feeling lonely and misunderstood. No one knew the agonizing pain I felt being trapped in my thoughts and anger. I was becoming my biggest threat. I was starving for comfort. I would reach for it, get close yet never touch it. I never really felt deserving of comfort anyway.

I was always fighting, running, and seeking safety. I was lost and had no direction. I was tired of fighting myself out of the constant prison I lived in. Going through the motions, working, and doing for others while I waited for someone to do for me.

I had no idea that my experiences had anything to do with my past. That the way I was acting was how I coped with the pain of numerous disappointments, betrayals, and the unmanageable abuse I lived through. The self-harming behaviors I learned while living at Lucy's felt lifesaving at times. When I was angry at them, I would take it out on myself.

It was as though inflicting physical pain on myself, took the focus away from the unmanageable emotional pain I often experienced.

At other times, it was the self-harming action that bought me back and helped me feel. I was so far gone and dreaded returning.

I do not recall exactly where I met Beth. Perhaps we met at my first social work-related internship, Jewish Board for Children and Families, Inc. She became a good friend. She encouraged me to volunteer at The Door: A Center for Alternatives, a program in downtown Manhattan that worked with troubled adolescents. Beth knew that the way to get ahead in the social work field or any other one, for that matter, was by having experience. I thought it was odd to work without pay but she spoke about it as though it was the smart thing to do. I needed to stay busy anyway as idle time had a way of making me anxious.

In years to come, I would get better at creating time to rest and be quiet. But back then, quiet time could fire up the memories of the past. I had questions about why things happened the way they did and what I may have done to provoke or deserve it. Sometimes, remembering that God was also taking care of me and sending me angels such as Myra, Veronica, my sister Zulema, Cesar and Beth would calm the anxiety. But the thoughts, memories and feelings of horror, fear, anger, and sadness did not dwindle for many years.

I took Beth's suggestion and together we went to The Door and applied for volunteer jobs. After the application process and request of references they stated they would get back to us. I left there concerned about whether I had done the right thing by applying at such a place. I wondered if they wanted to know more about my history because I would be working with children. The other jobs I had gotten only wanted to check references from my previous jobs. These folks wanted to know if I had ever committed a crime. I had not told Beth about my experience at the group home. I did not want her to think I was a bad person, be afraid of me and not want to be my friend. Besides, it was embarrassing to share with her why I had ended up at such a place.

Beth and I were invited to return to volunteer at The Door. Later in our relationship, after Beth had shared information about her family, I finally shared with her how concerned I had been about my past coming up in the background check.

"Girl, you shouldn't feel bad about that. I too am an incest survivor. Getting abused was not our fault and you shouldn't feel ashamed!"

As I said the term, "incest survivor," I wondered what it meant? I asked Beth.

I knew that the many things that happened at Lucy's house and the way I was treated was not right. But I was shocked to know that there was a term for what happened. I was sexually abused. Beth shared with me that childhood sexual abuse was quite common and that being sexually abused by a family member made it incest.

My talks with Beth marked the beginning of my understanding of my behavior and how my experiences had affected me. Throughout our many talks, the idea that she had experienced sexual abuse and did not blame herself was most relieving. It was also helpful to know that she was a decent person. I did not think she was weird, a sicko, deserving of abuse. I thought she was cool. At times, I tried to believe the same about myself.

Beth inspired me to read and learn more about childhood sexual abuse and how to help myself. It opened me up to a world of healing I did not know was possible. It gave me hope that the voices would quiet down and the feelings of disgust and fear would cease.

Ironically, the position that I got at The Door was that of a Sexual Health and Awareness Volunteer Counselor. The kids at The Door were rough kids, the type I had encountered the year I lived at the group home. I must admit that these teenagers were light years ahead of me. I learned a lot in my attempt to educate them. I had information on the public services available to them, where to get contraception, abortions, and STD tests. They had real life experiences, experimenting, and exploring their sexuality and sexual selves. The greatest gift was becoming more and more comfortable with my body and talking about sex, which later allowed me to talk about my experiences as a survivor of sexual abuse and incest.

My friend Beth introduced me not only to the Center for Alternatives but also to my first 12-Step program. At the time, she often talked about her childhood. Her mother had been diagnosed with mental health issues and her father was an alcoholic.

I was getting used to telling anyone who wanted to know the horror that my life had been. We shared our war stories all the time.

"You know Santa, you should really consider coming with me to a meeting some time. If it were not for these meetings, I would be as crazy as my mother," Beth said one day.

Beth was convinced that the meetings would help me address the issues with my family.

"Your mood swings, your depression, your issues with your attachment to your husband and your co-dependency. The whole thing about you always feeling like a victim. That and your uncontrollable anger are all things I can relate to. This is the way we act because we grew up in violence and chaos and what they call dysfunctional families. There are meetings for adult children of alcoholics. Their program is called ACOA. (Adult Child of Alcoholics) "

"There are also meetings to help people overcome codependency called CODA (Codependency Anonymous). You seem quite codependent."

Beth explained these terms and went on to share what these meetings were all about and how she had found them to be helpful. I would do just about anything to feel better.

I liked Beth. She was a red-headed Jewish woman and was cool. She took the 12-Step meeting thing seriously and was always talking about it, trying to recruit me. The next time she went to a meeting, I went with her. It did not take me long to realize that I was an adult child of an alcoholic, among other things. Before I knew it, I found myself attending the meetings.

I felt like I finally belonged somewhere. This was a place where I was not the only intense, sensitive, and weird one. I had found a place where I was understood and could be myself. In time, I allowed all my selves to show up. I did not like the idea of having character defects but I certainly had them. These were parts of my behavior I could not control or explain.

The structure and repetitiveness of the program provided me with the consistency I yearned for. Although I did not always want or welcome it, I soon found that I needed it. Like love, every muscle, bone, and cell of my body sang its praises.

Another unexpected piece was how much they talked about and emphasized God. They referred to it as, "the God of your understanding." I knew about God. I had grown up in an environment where God was spoken about often but usually in very conflicting ways. Often it was my mother who talked about

God as a friend, Father, someone who would keep you safe or punish you, especially if you did not behave according to my mother's standards. On the other hand, my father spoke about God as someone you should fear like we feared him or someone who was to blame for all the discord and challenges he experienced. And then there were these movies on television, particularly during Easter, which portrayed a God who had a son called Jesus. Jesus looked nothing like anyone in my family even though they claimed we were created in His image. I decided that at some point, I would figure it all out. For now, I just knew that something or someone had saved my butt many times.

Knowing that I would and could identify and develop a relationship with a God of my understanding was very comforting to me. The people in CODA and ACOA said that what was important was knowing that there was a power greater than me and any other human being. A power that could take care of the things I could not. A power that was interested in all of me including my crazies. A power that would never abandon me.

I am not sure I totally trusted this power or that I knew what kinds of things to release to it but I did believe there was a power greater than me. But why did it allow Lucy and Carlos to do all these horrible things to me?

The 12-Step recovery programs also stressed taking things one step at a time.

They'd often say at the end of the meetings, "It works if you work it. So, bring a lot of love and don't give up."

There were other sayings they would chant like a mantra at the end of meetings.

"What you hear here, let it stay here."

"Take what works and leave the rest."

I could easily write a book on the popular sayings or as they referred to them, the 12 step "slogans" alone. These slogans have saved me throughout the years. They were ingrained in my thoughts and popped up when I least expect it to help me through a challenging time. I remain grateful.

12-step programs also teach members about something called, "The Promises." I learned that some promises can be realized and some dreams can come true. The notion that I could make peace with my body had not yet become a conscious desire nor did I think it was a dream that might come true. One day I became aware that it was not so much about making peace with my body but becoming aware that I had a body which I could learn to love. I would look at myself in the mirror and the feeling would arise that perhaps I could learn to love my body. First it was from a distance. As I got closer to the mirror, a different feeling—judgment—would come in. What had seemed acceptable changed. The thoughts began to spiral downward.

I was too fat. I had too many stretch marks, particularly on the belly. But those stretch marks were part of a belly that had given birth to me. A belly that had to be cut open in the process of finding myself. My thighs, hands, and legs—though strong—were skinny. Looking at those darkened knees and elbows, I thought they were worn. And the scars on my legs and arms looked like a body that had been at war. That same body had served as a shield, a great shield that protected my vulnerable organs and fragile parts. The parts of me I thought had gotten me in trouble also held the experiences I could no longer deny.

My body held painful memories. It reminded me of my struggles and failures. I used to see my body as a symbol of my weakness, lack of discipline, confusion, conflict, shame, and disgust. My skinny legs that were smaller than the rest of my body had been laughed at and ridiculed. The remainder of my round body guaranteed I would not be misread, misunderstood, or judged as a sexual object. My mother said being round was a sign of wealth vs. starvation. I asked myself if I could get rid of the fatty areas on my inner thighs and allow myself to feel vulnerable. I wondered if I could give up the protection the extra weight afforded me. In time, I could and would.

I learned to tell myself, "You are safe. Believe it." I would also repeat the affirmations: "I am safe. I am safe to release the old patterns. Safe to say those are not my truths."

As I healed, the cravings for the sweetness in candy, sugar and high carbohydrates diminished. On a conscious level, I knew there would never be enough of those foods to fill the void I sometimes experienced. I could have it all—the sweetness, someone loving and honoring me, whatever that meant for me on any given day. Somewhere I read that the metaphysical condition of diabetes is a need for sweetness, joy, and happiness. No surprise that I would end up with type II diabetes. The idea that excessive amounts of sugar could make me happy was not true. I realized the time had come to let go, to be free to experience true sweetness, joy, and happiness. What a head trip I had put myself through.

Over time I would begin to celebrate the strength, softness and beauty of my hands and feet. My feet had been around and gotten me around. I developed a sense of respect, gratitude, and compassion for my body. I saw myself with my big shoulders that were open to the world. I saw myself opening my heart, seeing my angelic face, dimpled cheeks, and piercing eyes. Some days, I was able to celebrate what my soul's mirror reflected. The love within the true beauty. The beauty I came to see.

These were the seeds of my healing journey. I began to feel it was time for me to do something different with my life. To stop hanging out, drinking and smoking pot. I had gotten my Associate Degree from LaGuardia Community College and without skipping much more than a beat, I registered for advanced studies at Hunter College. I had been told the next thing was getting a bachelor's degree. Why not keep going?

Married life with Cesar continued. Beth and I had had conversations about codependency and I knew that her observations were not incorrect. I understood what she meant when she described me that way. Often, I felt that in a fundamental way, my relationship with Cesar was off kilter. I took care of him emotionally, economically, physically, and of course, the womanly way. I liked that he, in turn, had lots of dreams and expectations. Whether or not I understood it then, I expected him to be responsible for my happiness, even when I did not know what it would take for me to be happy.

Cesar brought little to our relationship. I got him his first decent job at the elevator factory. It was me who got myself indebted every year so that we could go to Ecuador. Later, I paid for him to go on his own. As a liberal couple, we decided it was good for him to go visit his family and friends without me sometimes. I had very few friends of my own. I did all my social things with him and he did most of his socializing with me. That was unless he was hanging out with the guys and would let me know he would be out late or maybe not come home at all. All I asked was that he call and let me know he was safe.

To all of that, Beth would tell me, "That's not you being liberal and modern, that's you being an enabler, enabling him to keep drinking and hoping he will change for you."

I knew she was right, as hard as it was to hear it. It was time for me to address my issues. I had to start somewhere. I needed to be proactive about healing, one step at a time.

Beth asked me if I was interested in going with her to an Ashram in upstate New York. She wanted to hear her guru, Guru Maya, speak. They were having a Satsang, a Hindu spiritual gathering that included a special lecture and sacred chanting. I was grateful for her suggestion. I knew very little about all this but had a fascination with the Hare Krishnas, who I remembered seeing when I was a kid. They were always parading down 84th Street, chanting and playing music. We all thought they were weird, probably because they were different. Fanatics we called them. I was attracted to them. I admired their dedication to whatever it was they believed in. I really liked the music, particularly the Hindi drumming.

We talked all the way during our drive upstate. We compared our experiences and talked about what Beth referred to as her, "character defects," meaning the crazy ways she acted. We ate potato chips and popcorn. It was the first time I heard that mixing them made a good combination and they did. We listened to and chanted along with New Age music.

On that beautiful, crisp, early Fall Day, the trees created a magical landscape of vibrant crimsons, oranges, yellows, greens, and blacks. Fall in upstate New York was one of the most incredibly amazing things I had ever seen. As we arrived at the Ashram, we drove through the open fields with green pastures and huge trees. Then out of nowhere a big, old, red-brick building came into view, with gigantic stained-glass windows. The impressive, double doors which opened outward, reminded me of the doors of old cathedrals I had seen on television in places like Jerusalem.

Inside the building, all the wood and marble created a special kind of beauty. The moment the door opened; people lined up. Though there must have been hundreds of people, I was taken by the silence of the space. It was a quality of quietness and peace only found in a sacred place. We walked towards an open assembly hall where we would meet Guru Maya, the Hindu Spiritual teacher who would bless us with her wisdom and Shakti or spiritual energy.

In the large, open space, a sweet incense burned which I later learned was Nag Champa. Nag Champa is used in most Hindu sacred spaces and was to become one of my favorites. Brightly lit candles, a beautiful armed chair with a wide, tall back, sat on the stage. The chair was covered in a rich, royal blue velvet fabric, fit for only a very loved and revered spiritual teacher.

I can only say that meeting Guru Maya inspired an overwhelming feeling of reverence in me. Not only was she beautiful in every way but she also exuded an energy of peace and joy.

She spoke of developing a practice of honoring and loving oneself and others. By the time I went to the Ashram, I had participated in many Catholic church services; I was raised Catholic. I had found them boring and went more out of admiration for the architecture than the sermon, which usually went over my head and nowhere near my heart. As a kid I would go as a chore, my mother was good at sending the kids to church out of guilt and obligation or to get rid of us.

Guru Maya spoke in a calm, clear voice, and an easy-to-follow style. I felt like she was talking specifically to me. It was glorious. I believe everyone there had the same response to hearing her. I could feel her love for us all and no doubt the people who were present all loved her. She spoke about quieting our minds and feeling the innate peace we all were. She encouraged us to do and expect good things and stressed the importance of starting wherever you are and setting an intention to purify your body, mind, and spirit. She talked about us being a combination of what we think, say, and put into our body.

That event was my introduction to meditation and the idea that I could control my thoughts, hence my life. The call-and-response chanting united us all in one voice. After her two-hour talk, she blessed each person who came to her while live musicians played chants and other spiritual music. Then we were invited to the cafeteria where they offered us a small, "Prasad," a dessert-like treat that had been blessed by Guru Maya. We had herbal tea and the opportunity to visit with old and new friends. Beth and I shared about our experience. I was so grateful she had invited me. I was on a natural high, the type that does not fade quickly like pot and does not trigger the munchies. I left wanting more.

I appreciated Beth. With her I felt comfortable and safe. We both were ready to make changes in our lives and figure ourselves out. I had been given a second chance to create a better life experience and I wanted to do just that. I'd read many books and explored many popular self-help suggestions. I was clear that I could not change my past experiences. I could, however, alter the way the past impacted my future life.

Beth was on this journey as well, in the fast lane to healing, always doing, or exploring something that kept her moving. She attended workshops, day and weekend retreats and lectures. She was willing to share them all with me. I followed in her footsteps and often joined her. When she invited me to Kripalu, a Yoga and Meditation Center in Lenox, Massachusetts for a Yoga retreat, I jumped at the chance. By then, I had been practicing Yoga at home on my own. I did the "asanas," postures and the "pranayama" yogic breathing practices. I had been inspired by a book I found by chance, about losing thirty pounds in thirty days by following a particular yoga routine. Different but enjoyable, Yoga kept me hopeful about losing weight. Uncontrolled eating to avoid or numb or alter my moods was something that I had struggled with for many years.

I have often said that many of my most rewarding experiences have come when I was just going along. At eight-teen-years old, a bachelor's degree in hand, I was at my first official social work job.

Who would've thought I would one day have a job I enjoyed, one where I supported and helped others? At Sanctuary for Families, I was surrounded by women who knew what they wanted to do and better yet, knew they were entitled. This was my first time working with or even hearing about women who considered themselves feminist. The idea of women's rights and women's empowerment made sense to me. We are as capable as men and deserve the same respect. Why not?

Every afternoon over lunch, the whole staff, ten of us, would sit together and have conversations about our lives. My fellow staff members were encouraging and inviting. I was new to the group and not sure of what was appropriate to share about my life. I listened and often talked about my experiences at work.

Of all the staff, I was most intrigued by a young, white, lanky, red-headed woman named Samantha. We were around the same age but Samantha seemed so sure about what she wanted to do with her life. I might've been a little jealous. It was clear she was smart; empowered and knew she was entitled. She was on the eccentric side and wore raggedy overalls, sneakers, and tee shirts to work. Her face was make-up free and her hair was styled in Nubian knots. She ate raw broccoli, cauliflower, and green juice that she called shots. She was different but there was something about Samantha I found attractive.

I perked up when Samantha started a discussion about going to graduate school for social work. In two years, Samantha planned to have her graduate degree, take the New York State licensing exam, and become a certified Social Worker. Everyone was excited for her and spoke as though it was the normal thing to do at her age. I could see that for Samantha and all the other white women around the table, going to graduate school was a no-brainer. It was an easy goal for a group of privileged white feminists but was it possible for little old me?

I wondered if I had what it took to go to social work school. Would they accept me even though I was a high school dropout and had only a GED? Would my bachelor's degree be enough? Would they ask and what would I tell them about my family background?

"Santa, Santa." I heard the ladies saying from a distance, "You know, the application process is still open." "Why don't you consider applying?"

"You'd really make a good Social Worker," our Executive Director said.

"Really, you think I'd be accepted?"

"Well, you'll never know unless you apply."

The next thing I knew, Samantha was giving me the website address to Hunter College School of Social Work. She encouraged me to complete the application process as soon as possible. She mentioned that the deadline was quickly approaching.

Without giving it much thought, I took her suggestion and completed the application, listed my references, and wrote the essay; Given my undergraduate degree from Hunter College the rest of the application process went smooth. I had never thought about being a social worker. My childhood dream had been to be an attorney so I could represent my brothers when they got into difficulties with the law. I also thought about becoming a Correctional Officer. The only type of social worker I knew about were the ones who worked for Child Protective Services. They specialized in taking kids away and sending them to group homes. The other social workers I was familiar with worked with juvenile delinquents or at the welfare office. This perception was based on the experiences from my childhood. I would later learn more about social work as a profession.

As was my habit, I went along with the idea and the required steps. As I went through the application process, I got excited. The essay I wrote reflected my genuine desire to help and support others. It also gave me hope that even though I had not yet been able to make a difference in my family, I could help others.

Several weeks later over lunch, Samantha shared details about her interview at Hunter College. She expected to get her acceptance letter along with the necessary materials and invitation to the New Student Seminar.

"Hey Santa, how was your interview?" Someone asked.

"My interview? I never got an interview appointment."

Samantha got all worked up. "Oh no! I believe this is the last day for the group interviews. I'm surprised you didn't get an appointment."

"I don't know why I didn't get an appointment." I said.

I felt a little defensive. Were they implying I was irresponsible or that I had done something wrong? In retrospect, I probably felt disappointed and a little embarrassed.

What I have come to know about myself is, before embarking on a healing process, whenever I felt threatened, whether real or perceived, my reaction was to go into fight response. I also learned that human beings and particularly trauma survivor's neurological threat responses are fight, flight or freeze. These responses are coded in our DNA via a survival of the fittest consciousness. Over time, especially when there has been a history of multiple traumas, habitual responses to threat develop. People with unresolved trauma might react neurologically or on a physical level and will seek resolution through responses and behaviors that keep one alive at any cost, even when there is no threat to speak of. I've learned that the body remembers every experience we've ever had – good, bad, or indifferent. Hence, triggers can come from an actual/present threat, imagined, remembered, from the past, present or even the future. And only when we are regulated, (feeling safer) can we begin to identify the actual threat, its validity, and the actions necessary to regain a sense of safety.

The day the conversation about my college application took place, I almost blew it. I could not understand why these women were making such a big deal of these graduate school interview. A couple of the women had gotten on the phone in a sincere attempt to support me. It felt like things were happening in slow motion. It was then I realized that these women were on my side. One of them came back and said they confirmed it was not too late to get an interview. I just had to get across town to Hunter College Graduate School of Social Work in the next couple of hours.

"Santa, you've got to be quick. This is the last group interview," another of them hollered.

There I was, just having an ordinary day. Jeans, loafers, a basic blouse, hair in a bun, no make-up and the polish on my nail's half gone. There was no way I could make it home to Queens and back to Hunter College in a couple of hours. I was already feeling awkward, stupid, and irresponsible. I could not show up looking like a mess and make a fool of myself.

My mind went to the past. I wondered again why they did not send me an appointment. I wondered if this was a sign that graduate school was not for me. I confirmed that they had gotten my application. I dealt with my financial aid and secured a loan to pay for school. Why was this happening?

I was going downhill quickly. I knew this place well; feeling sorry for myself and creating a story of how nothing ever went well for me. How I was all alone and there was never anyone there to help me.

One of the ladies brought me out of feeling sorry for myself. "Come on, Santa."

While I was processing, they had been talking out a plan. I must have told them I was uncomfortable going to the interview in what I was wearing. Next thing I knew they were calling me to the donation room. We kept a donation room with clothing and accessories for women and children who were victims of domestic violence.

"You can't miss the last day of the interviews, Santa. We'll make sure you get there."

It was hard to take it all in. But it was time to get into gear and make this thing happen. I dried my tears and went to the donation room. The women had picked out an outfit for me.

I wore a black pleated skirt and plaid jacket, pumps, no stockings, and a hideous broach. I might have looked ridiculous but I was on my way. I took a deep breath and tried to calm myself. I found myself in a cab and on the way to Hunter College. To my surprise, I was not along and there was plenty of help.

Once there, I let go of the fact that I looked out of place. To my surprise, no one cared or even noticed. They were expecting me and invited me to sit. Six or eight of us were in attendance and one woman conducted the interview. A short while later, I was engaged in an interesting conversation about being a social worker. I talked about how I knew it was what I wanted to do even before I knew there was such a thing.

I shared how I wanted to help others, how I wished there had been someone to help me and my family as we navigated immigrating to the US.

That day, in the group interview at Hunter College, I realized what I really wanted was to understand why my family was so screwed up. Getting my letter of acceptance into Hunter College would be a day of celebration both at home with Cesar and at the office. Thanks to the women at the battered women's agency, I was on my way, again, to a whole new life.

Social Work school opened the door to a new world. I managed to attend school while still working at Sanctuary for Families. I enjoyed all my classes, except for Statistics. Yet, to my surprise I even excelled in that class. I chose many of my classes based on what I felt I needed to understand about some aspect of my life. At times, it was sad to identify or over-identify but mostly I came away feeling hopeful.

Connections, support, and friendships developed quickly. It felt great to belong. I took in the material and was able to apply it to my own experience. With each class, I got a better understanding of what happened in my family. I developed a better sense of who I was and how my past had affected my future.

Social Work and Homelessness was one of the classes I registered for with the intent of understanding another aspect of my life. The issue of homelessness was a lot more complex than I thought. Ironically, for some it was a choice and they were not all mentally ill. Some of them were quite eloquent.

They were lawyers, doctors, fathers, and mothers. They spoke to me about their dreams, struggles and challenges. They shared their disgust with the social system, religion, and God and how they had failed them. Some of them were in fact mentally ill and battled with addictions.

I gained a great deal of respect for homeless people. Yes, some of them were repulsive and even scary. Some stunk and at times their smell turned my stomach. But they were also interesting, funny, and caring. And they wanted and needed their story to be told.

From the day I saw and talked to my brother while we were out doing field studies, my relationship with him changed. After that day, I no longer hid from or avoided him. Luisito was my eldest brother. And yes, he suffered with Schizophrenia, but his mental illness never stopped me from loving him.

Throughout the years, I had also struggled with my relationship with my mother. That struggle was apparent at every point in our relationship. My yearning for my mother's attention. My anger towards her for not protecting me. My blaming her for my sexual abuse. If she had not been selfishly and irresponsibly focused on her own life, I would not have ended up at Lucy's house.

The litany of her failings seemed endless. I dealt with all these disappointments by vowing to go to any length to take care of myself. I was determined to not let my dysfunctional family interfere with the life I had worked so hard to put together.

I often heard in my thoughts, "They took my childhood away but they will not take away my future by bringing their craziness into my life."

That said, I loved my mother and always had compassion for her. With a great deal of inner work, I came to understand why she made the decisions she made. Leaving my father, exploring her sexuality, and seeking happiness. I forgave her for all of it. However, when she needed a place to stay because my brother Luis had started yet another fire smoking in bed or when my brother Daniel had gotten into a mess with dangerous people, the truth was, I wanted nothing to do with them or her.

I did offer to support her. After all, she was my mother. I felt sorry for her. In her mid-fifties, she looked and probably felt like she was seventy. She also had serious health concerns. I was willing to take a risk and offer her a place to live until we figured out a better plan but my mom loved her boys, particularly her Luisito. Helping my mother was a complex, package deal.

When I would have the occasional visit with her, she would say, "You guys are siblings. I did not bring you up to hate each other."

"Mama, you can live with me but you can't have Luisito staying here. I do not want the drama. I do not want him coming around insisting to be let in, banging on the door, hollering, and cussing all times of the day or night. I do not want him coming here insisting that he be let in along with all his stuff. I don't want to have to call the police when he freaks out if you don't give him what he wants."

That is what I would say to her while my heart raced and my resentments increased. I wondered why she put me in that awkward position. Had she not done enough harm already? My mother was one of those people I felt sad about and angry with at the same time. And I felt guilty for feeling that way.

I would not fall for it again. Next time she would need to go to an assisted living place. Next time I would choose me. I would protect my home and family, that is what I told myself.

"Why do you feel you have to put up with him? He's a grown man and he should get help." I told her.

I came to understand that Luisito was her son, her first born. She would never abandon him, even if it led to her living in an assisted living or nursing home. Wherever my mother was, Luisito was. He would always find her and she would always be relieved and glad to see him. I came to understand that her relief and joy was equal to the amount of fear and worry she experienced when she did not hear from him.

Social work school and particularly the homelessness class were a divine intervention. I developed a better understanding of my mother's pain, turmoil and how conflicted she must have felt. No wonder she was so proficient at making me feel guilty and irresponsible. It was probably a projection of how she felt about herself.

Over time I found a way to be in my mother's life, which meant being in my brother's life. We would run into him; he was always roaming around. He knew his Mama would give him a few dollars, cigarettes, and food.

My mother wondered how I was going to handle Luisito showing up at the nursing home. My interactions with him in that space and time were different. I had a better understanding of his experience. We discussed how things were going in his homeless world.

"Did you figure out which is the best soup kitchen in town? Do you have a church where you can go and get a shower?" I would ask him.

I could feel my mother watching me. I was talking with my brother as opposed to avoiding him. I could tolerate his craziness.

"How about we go and get some Chinese food?" I would ask my brother.

"Are you going to get me some Egg Foo Young," Luisito would immediately ask.

"Whatever you want," I would say.

We would walk to the takeout restaurant, holding hands with each other, my mother grinning from ear to ear.

"Go ahead, tell mom what we discussed the last time I saw you. The deal we made."

"We are going to get our food and take it to the little park down the street to eat. Cucuta said she would take me to Chinese when and if I show up clean. If not, it's takeout."

"That's right." I said, as we all laughed.

We had an understanding. My mother could see that something had changed. I was no longer intimidated by his illness. It was not about being a bad sister.

It was about setting appropriate boundaries and not being an enabler. I got that although he was not well, he had the capacity, particularly when he was adhering to his medication regimen, to show up decently and without the drama. As my mom observed us interacting and negotiating our relationship, I sensed that she had gained respect and appreciation for me.

Mom and I conversed about mental illness and the importance of her not enabling her sons anymore. We talked about Luisito having some responsibility for being out on the street, even if it was from not advocating for himself, taking suggestions, or allowing others to help him. I shared with my mom some of the things I had learned at the Homelessness class. I told her about the programs available for people like Luisito. I told her there were shelters, soup kitchens, public showers, and medical attention.

I told her that Luisito knew how to access these services and that he needed to follow the rules. The most important rule being taking his medication. I also explained the social services system to her. I remember her face relaxing as she wrapped her head around the idea that there were options and help for her child.

Mom and I started talking about Alanon. We discussed the primary concepts of Alanon, a twelve-step program that provided support and guidance to the family and spouses of alcoholics. Alanon gave us hope. My mother and I loved going to the early morning meeting downtown. She got to talk about the challenges of having a son with mental illness, others addicted to drugs and an ex-spouse who was an alcoholic. Through that process we came to understand each other so much more. We also learned to respect and honor our individual needs. Gradually, we began to heal our relationship while hanging out and having the predictable coffee and donuts they always had at Alanon meetings.

I grew to have great respect for my mother and her respect for me grew as well. I understood her love for her sons and how challenged she was. I also came to terms with her depression and the hardships she faced throughout her life.

The two of us, along with Luisito, regularly hung out at the local park, went to the movies, and ate out at the takeout Chinese restaurant.

I came to realize that I could let go of the fear that my mother, brother, and family were going to show up in my life and create havoc. I could let go of the fear that somehow what I had created for myself, safety and consistency, would be contaminated and ruined. I could let go of the guilt, the guilt about moving on and creating a better life. I realized that I had a right to a better life.

I came to understand this did not make me selfish or a bad daughter or sister. I got that I could have an integrated life, one that included my family of origin. I did not want to be the person my mother was. I did not want to repeat the same patterns I grew up with. I knew that I would be different from them and that I would create a new story.

Part II

We must let go of the life we have planned, so as to accept the one that is waiting for us.

~Joseph Campbell

12
Learning to Love Me... First

Cesar and I had been maintaining our marriage for nearly thirteen years. He was my savior, the man I once referred to as my God. The man who helped me heal my wounds of trauma, betrayal and lies. I trusted him. I had shared all that had happened to me with him and never once felt judged or shamed. In fact, he seldom said much. I told him what my sister and her husband had done to me. I told him why I cried when I had an orgasm. I told him why I do not visit my family, why I lived in an adult group house and why I was sent to an adolescent group home, along with many other stories.

Usually, he had nothing to say. Sometimes I thought he was overwhelmed by the events of my life or that he was not interested or not taking me seriously. I thought maybe he thought I was crazy, made it all up or deserved it. Other times I felt his love and support.

I wondered if my marriage to Cesar was what I needed at the time. Someone that belonged to me and would keep me safe. Cesar promised to be my friend. He believed in my goodness. I did not ask for much, I just wanted him to want me. He had a family and that meant I too had a family. He loved his sisters and mother, so that automatically made him a good man. They say if a man loves his mother, he will make a good husband.

I had experienced a lot of devastation, betrayal, and disappointments throughout my life, especially as a child. I had experienced being a child lost in the world, alone and without guidance, no true connections or attachment to anyone. In Cesar, I found a friend and not just a friend but a friend that I grew up with. I became whole. I became a woman. Cesar was willing to be with me in my brokenness. I had gotten my GED, gotten a family, a home, guidance, even learned about basic grooming.

I remember Cesar saying to me, "Santa, put lotion on those ashy elbows and knees. Hell, I did not know I needed to put lotion on my body. I thought lotion was for little babies. When my face was ashy, my mother didn't say, "go put some lotion on it," she would take some spit and rub it on my eyebrows or whatever. As time went on, I would laugh every time I thought of this. I came to understand that this was not just typical of some Dominican mothers, but true of lots of Latin moms.

Cesar and I were at a particularly good place in our lives. We had recently purchased our very first brand new little red car, a four-door Dodge. We had a nice apartment in Queens, the perfect apartment, freshly painted, pretty pinewood floors, washer, and dryer. We lived right across from a beautiful park. I had lost weight and could wear a size fourteen again. I had just gotten my graduate degree.

I had been working at Sanctuary for Families as a counselor, my first job as a master level Social Worker. I had gotten promoted and was now the Director of the Counseling Department. I was making more money than I ever had. I worked with a group of feminists who were clear about women's empowerment. I was big into being independent and liberal. This was the beginning of the rest of my life.

To top it off, I had just started a part-time private practice with my school friend, Nicole. Cesar and I would often discuss our dreams. Cesar wanted to move to Venezuela and open a children's orphanage. I planned to be right there with him.

Cesar wanted to take up running for his health. As always, I would support him. If he wanted to be a vegetarian, I would stop eating meat. If he wanted to stay out all night, that was fine with me. Wasn't life perfect? Yes, my husband drank excessively but so what?

At some point the truth about my situation hit me like a bolt of lightning. The truth: Cesar was doing whatever he wanted to do including having affairs with other women. He said I had become his mother and his sister. He loved me and did not want to hurt me any longer. He wanted to leave our marriage and set us both free. As hard as I tried to give him space and take good care of him, I had been smothering him. He said he could no longer tolerate my codependent behaviors. Him having affairs, lying, and taking advantage of me was not the problem. The problem was that I had become his mother and sister. I took care of him and made very few requests. All I wanted was for him to love and not hurt me. Apparently, that was too much to ask.

It was over. There was nothing I could do, my heart ached. My mind was overwhelmed and it felt like my life was over. I didn't know where to turn or couldn't imagine going on. I was too cowardly to end my life and too hurt and lost to continue. My best friend, the savior who had helped me heal my wounds had joined the list of those who lied to and betrayed me.

At that time in my life, loving me meant not rejecting me. I would later decide that he had left me because he loved me. He wanted me to have a man who would be good to me. He wanted me to learn how to take care of and love myself more than I loved him.

He left me with a few words of wisdom. "Never love someone else more than you love yourself and never make another individual your God."

These were phrases he often told me when we were together. I thought, man, how humble is he? That is why I loved him so much. He left no room for any further rationalization or denial. He was gone. He wanted nothing to do with our marriage and was convinced that a do over would not be possible.

"You will never forgive me or trust me again. "It will never be the same and you don't deserve the pain of giving me another chance. When we got married, I needed a green card and I thought, why not marry Santa? As time went on, I learned how to love you. Your care, understanding and compassion were comforting and a soft, and what seemed like, an easy place to land, but I was not in love with you." He went on to explain what he met by, "I had become his mother, his sister". I did not allow him to care for me. I had no expectations of him, I allowed him to use me, and he could not love me the way a man loves a woman, without wondering if this was the night I would have some memory. Santa, He told me on the way out. You're a great woman and I am sorry to hurt you.

I was devastated. I was losing the man who had once told me, "Get some new underwear. You don't have to wait until they are falling apart to get new ones." I figured, what difference did it make, no one would see them anyway.

I couldn't get him to agree to go to therapy, move out of the country or pretend nothing had happened. I had to process the shock of it all alone. I was prepared to give him more time, to beg him to try a little harder and pretend his wrongdoing was a mistake. I had a lot of experience fantasizing and dissociating. I could create any story I needed to survive. He did not trust or believe that I could forgive him. He walked away and stayed away. After a short time of begging and trying to bargain, fighting to stay in denial, I got it. This relationship was over and there was nothing I could do to change that.

Unable to see through the tears or feel past the sorrow, I was not good for much. Everything reminded me of him, of the 13 years we were together. People wondered why I was not angry with him. But how can you be angry at the person who claimed to love you for so long. He was the man who accepted the broken me, that helped me heal the open wounds years of abuse had left behind. How could I be angry at the person who gave me purpose and hope, who encouraged me to strive for love and joy? How could I be angry at the person who so often comforted me when I experienced a flash back while he made love to me? Or when I got overwhelmed by the fact that sex and sexual pleasure were not always accompanied by pain? Despite his deceit, my heart appreciated him for the many years we shared. After all, he was the best partner I ever had.

I turned to food and work to cope with the sorrow. I worked the pain away, focused on other people's pain and confusion. When I went home or shall I say before I got home, I would stop at the corner pizza shop and buy a large order of eggplant parmesan and a whole, cheesed Italian bread. I ate the same thing for dinner for over a month. I always promised to save some for lunch but I never found it to be enough to fill the void. I kept hoping that the hot spicy tomato sauce and eggplant and the stringy, fatty cheese would do it. I guess I made the eggplant parmesan my new God and the pizza shop my shrine.

Throughout my life, I had experimented with many different diets and weight loss programs. Everything from eating caramel candies called Adys and drinking teas that made you go to the bathroom, to taking unprescribed illegal pills and shots that promised to take your appetite away. Then I got into colonics, fasting, eating only certain types of foods, blending my foods, taking protein drinks, or only eating a candy bar for a meal. I read tons of books on how to lose weight. I did lose weight. What I did not get was how to keep it off and how to stop the compulsive eating. I read medical, nutritional, metaphysical and spiritual books on my relationship with food. What I learned later in life was that I had an addiction, I was a food addict.

I also joined a 12-step program which I have become incredibly grateful for. 12-Step programs for help with food issues, gave me a physical, mental, and spiritual solution to my uncontrollable eating. Throughout time I explored Overeaters anonymous followed by OA How and finally found Food Addicts in Recovery Anonymous or FA.

At some point, I realized that no amount of food was going to alleviate the ache I felt in my heart or clear the fog in my thoughts. I needed to move on. I needed to create a new life. I did not know where to begin. I did not know what to do first.

I needed help. I knew this was one thing I could not do on my own. After a short moment of reflection, my thoughts became truly clear. I needed to be in a place that was safe, a place that would help me understand what happened and make sense of it.

I knew where to go. I went to the Ashram, Kripalu in Lenox, Massachusetts. This was a place I was familiar with. A peaceful, easy, and beautiful place where I could just be. And as spirit would have it, they offered a program that would support me through this experience. I signed up for the 4-day retreat called, "Transformation through Transition." It was there I finally accepted the loss. I stopped wishing for something that no longer existed and had never been there.

After several days of processing, exploring, and experiencing my emotions which I found out were many but mostly sadness and sorrow, I came to a place where I felt peaceful. At times, I was incredibly sad, scared, confused, and disoriented. But now I felt a sense of grounding and security I had never felt. I knew that no matter how much pain I was experiencing, the hurt would eventually pass. I would be left with the opportunity to truly choose what I wanted to do with the rest of my life. I say truly choose because getting together with Cesar was a non-thought-out experience. When I met Cesar, I was in a vulnerable place. I had finally escaped the oppressive feeling that no matter where

I went, my perpetrators would find me. I had no contact with anyone in my family and had no friends, except for the ladies at the rooming house.

Thank God, by the time Cesar and I broke up I had been in therapy at least two years. I was grateful to my Human Behavior teacher at Social Work School for suggesting everyone in our class get a therapist.

Underneath all the challenging emotions there was a bit of excitement. Ironically, I was excited for myself and for my ex-husband. I was glad he was able to finally be honest with himself and consequently with me. I was glad to see him doing what he really wanted to do with his life without shame, guilt, and remorse. I felt gratitude for him. Yes, he was the cause of the pain I was experiencing at the time but he was also giving me the opportunity to create a whole new life.

When we first met, I was hurt, scared and angry, void of gratitude for anyone. When he left, I was hurt, scared and angry but full of gratitude for him, what we shared, all of which I experienced as loving and caring, empowering, growth producing and overall healing. I also felt gratitude for my life.

When I got back from the Ashram, I was ready to move on. I remember walking into the apartment that day and slowly opening the door. I was hoping he was not in the apartment and that he had done what we had agreed to.

Before I left, I told him, "I'm going away for a few days. When I return, I expect your stuff to be out of here."

I slowly opened the closet door. He was gone alright. The only thing he left was his bike.

During my years with Cesar, I learned how to love, care, and share my life with another person. Those years were also critical to learning about me. I was deeply hurt but I was not broken. I was ready for the next phase of my life. It was as though he chose this time to decide to leave because he knew I would be able to handle it now.

I had friends and family who supported me. But most of all I felt clear, open, and present. I felt close to God. I felt protected and knew that God had a plan for me. I remember standing there looking into the empty closet and remembering the day we went off to Niagara Falls. Suddenly, I did not feel lonely or abandoned. For the first time in my life, I was not a victim but a winner. Like what used to happen when I worked at the factory many years ago, I zoned out and zoned into the message, God's got you Ms. Santa. Don't ever forget that.

I grew up Catholic but not Spiritual. In those days, there seemed to be a major contradiction on when and how God showed up in our home. I understood that God was real. I knew that if you believed in God, you could experience a faith that would bring hope when you were hopeless and comfort when you despaired. I often heard my mother call on God for hope or comfort and for Him to take care of us, her children.

It was not unusual for us to ask my mother to ask God to bless us when we left her watch.

"La bendicion, mama!" The blessing, Mother!

I can hear my mother's response.

"Que Dios te bendiga. May God bless you."

When leaving home or going to sleep, we were taught to bless ourselves with the sign of the cross on our forehead, "the father, son and holy spirit." Ultimately, I outgrew the habit of drawing a cross on my forehead and asking others to bless me.

There had been times of despair and grief when I would walk into one of the ubiquitous cathedrals in New York City, which at the time, stood open for visitors. I saw God in the beauty of the space. I did not require religious rituals or representational figures.

The structure and energy of a church building had a calming effect. There was just God and me. No matter how heavy my heart, the space made me feel welcomed. The air was clear, crisp, and fresh. The dim and bright lights created perfect shadows and illuminated hidden treasures.

I could lose myself in the ceiling's amazing, intricate designs like labyrinths and yantras. I looked up and my aching head was calmed by the energy of the vast space. I talked to the Creator, asked for relief, and fantasized about the future. I prayed not necessarily for a time when I would have this or that but a time when I would feel peace and safety, serenity, and joy. Sometimes I would get an immediate sense of relief or the reassurance that no matter what was happening to disturb my peace, I was going to be okay.

As time went on, I learned that to feel this energy, I needed only to call on the spirit of God and focus my attention on the beautiful things around me. The Golden Altar, the statues of the saints, the glow of the burning candles, the stained-glass windows, the beautiful hanging lamps, and the marble floors. I just needed to notice the care and love that went into keeping the place clean, to know that this was a gift from God and a gift to God. Being there by myself made the Sunday service seem small by comparison. The rituals of getting on and off my knees seemed insignificant. Hearing the word of God from the priest seemed minor in comparison to the experience of hearing God's voice through the silence and the spirit of God itself, within me. I understood the true meaning of sacred space or holy space. I began to learn how to sit in silence and listen to that small voice within, listen to the Goddess I've become.

When I was young, I never knew there were so many names for God. God was God and that was all there was to it. God was everything, I was told. Yet I was raised to just call him God and He was certainly male. Besides his gender, I had no idea what God looked like. I assumed he was White, as his son Jesus Christ was White. But that was about all I knew. Later I heard that we were created in God's image. I also knew that God was always present and presumably everywhere. As for his purpose, essentially, God was always watching over me. I understood from my early exposure to God, that He watched over me both to take care of me, as well as to punish me if I got out of line. There were also times where it seemed like God plain old forgot me. It seemed like God forgot whole families at times. What I got from witnessing how my parents related to God was that He was to be revered and feared but also could be cursed and blamed.

I have chosen to call God by many names. Mother, Father, Everything God, Great Mystery, Spirit, Energy, Universe, Magic, Creator, Tunkashila and other names.

To me the scripture, God is love, says it all—pure and unaltered loving kindness. I get today that God is not there just to take care of and fulfill my requests. God has been there to show me how to be with myself and others. Like my mother, I have derived hope and inspiration from my relationship with the Creator. I have come to believe that I come from a source much greater than any one thing, a source immeasurable and unlimited. This source wanted me to grow closer to its liking. I believe one of the reasons I have manifested as a human being at this time is to work towards becoming more God-like and that this is only possible by recognizing the many forms of God.

I witnessed my mother receiving blessings and hope because of calling on God. Today I am clear there has always been something watching over me. It was this seed of faith that kept me hoping for an easier, happier existence. I am grateful to my mother for her faith and for instilling in me an understanding of the magic of faith. I'm also thankful for her initiating in me a belief in a "Creator."

Thinking about my mother's faith reminds me of the many times I have been moved by other people's faith and devotion. My visit to Niagara Falls with my then husband Cesar and my friends Victor and Romeo, was one of those times when I could not deny the existence of an omnipotent force. Victor was a friend I met at LaGuardia Community College during my undergraduate studies. Victor was one of the gentlest, most handsome, and sophisticated men I had ever met. He dressed fashionably and wore only top of the line brand names.

Victor had a Wall Street banker's style with a hint of bohemia. I had never seen white, baby pink and sky-blue shirts so crisp and fresh, topped with beautiful ties and buttery leather shoes to match. He was always perfectly shaved and looked like he got his hair trimmed every day. He wore stunning masculine jewelry, diamond rings and watches and always carried a matching leather man bag. His nails were perfectly manicured and he used colognes that made a statement about pride, prestige, and class. He exuded health and fitness and was very conscious of his diet and health. Wherever he showed up, people would ask me who he was. Victor knew he looked like someone straight out of GQ Magazine and loved it. He and I would often joke about the many ladies drooling over him. Many of the women at school were jealous of me, thinking perhaps he was my boyfriend. It was fun hanging out with him and vicariously benefitting from all the heads we turned. But no, they were so wrong. He was very much in love with Romeo, his lover and dear friend who was another incredibly handsome guy. Together they made a powerful, dynamic couple. A perfect combination of beauty, class, intellect, status, and sweet spirit.

But this day, on our way to Niagara Falls, it was not a pretty scene. By then Victor had developed symptoms of full-blown AIDS. He had contracted HIV from Romeo. This was at the height of the HIV/AIDS epidemic in New York City. Everyone who contracted HIV faced a death sentence. The medical world had no clue and offered no hope to those suffering with the disease. So many were dying from the complications of the illness but many more were dying from the fear of stigma, depression and by suicide.

It had been several months since his diagnosis was confirmed. It hit him hard.

Victor could not deal with the feelings and thoughts of being what he saw as contaminating and going through a slow death. He attempted suicide several times, the last time hoping to complete it by trying to run his car off a bridge on his way to Jones Beach. Not only had he not succeeded, but he also ended up with several fractures, broken bones and would be confined to a wheelchair for the rest of his life.

Although he failed at taking his life, he succeeded at killing his spirit. Shortly after that, he stopped accepting visits at home, except occasionally from me. He stopped talking and eating and within a few months he weighed no more than a hundred pounds. His skeleton-like body was nearly paralyzed. His favorite thing for me to offer him was a warm washcloth on his arms and back, followed by moisturizing his skin. He often said it made him feel alive and less contaminating. He thanked me for not treating him with the fear and terror he experienced from so many others he interacted with.

"Why would God have me die this way? Where is God? And why has he abandoned me?"

He once asked me, "Will you help me end my life?"

To my surprise, as I have no idea where this response came from, I told him I would.

"But only after you have seen, done and experienced everything you can still physically experience. And only if you agree to stop trying to take your own life."

He agreed.

We decided that day that we would plan a trip to Niagara Falls. He had said the next two places he wanted to visit were Niagara Falls and Colombia, South America.

"I need to see as much of God as I can before I leave this world. And I want to see my mother one more time."

His mother lived in Colombia.

Our trip to Niagara Falls was a long and challenging drive from NYC. But between Cesar, Romeo and I, Victor's wish to go to Niagara Falls was fulfilled. The contrast of life and death, light and darkness was overwhelming to us all. We cruised alongside the falls. We laughed and cried like we would never do again.

The enormous falls, their roaring sound as they spilled into the river and into the ocean and the expression on Victor's face of peace and surrender, remained on my mind for years. We all agreed that God was real and was going to take care of him and us. That day, he saw God and we saw him seeing God. His body relaxed and he let go. He spoke about the beauty and power of the falls and thanked God for his life. He asked for His forgiveness.

"God, I offer myself to you, to do with me as you wish."

Our trip back home the next day was quite different then our trip up to Niagara Falls. We shared stories, jokes, laughter, and tears and planned our trip to Colombia.

Victor was free from the grip of HIV/AIDS. With God in his spirit and on his mind, his fears, and obsessions about ending his life ceased. Following this moment on it was as though he allowed God to hold him. Shame and disgust left him. He accepted that his life would probably be ending soon and decided to embrace the end of it.

"Help me to die in dignity." he said.

From that day on, our visits were quite different. During our visits, we talked about life and death and his fear of dying. He would often remind me that his fear was not of dying but of living with AIDS. He referred to all the wonderful experiences he had and how fortunate he had been to have lived a good life. He talked about his travels to Paris, France, Ethiopia, and Brazil. He shared stories about his experiences of love and beauty and just could not believe he was dying in such physical disgrace. We had conversations about who he wanted to say goodbye to, what he needed to put in order and most important to Victor, we began to plan his visit home to Colombia. I can see him embracing his mother. I can only imagine what that was like for him.

A few months after our overnight trip to Niagara Falls, Victor made his final trip back home to Columbia. Shortly after his trip to Columbia, Victor passed away. He died with God in his heart, gratitude for his life and in his mother's arms. Thank you, Victor, for your gift of faith.

People wondered why I was not angry and resentful about how Cesar and I ended. Instead, I was forgiving, loving and grateful. I did not understand it either. But over a period of time, it became very clear, Cesar had come into my life for a purpose. We got from each other and gave to each other what we needed at that time. Regardless of whether the time was right, I believed our coming together was. Cesar got a green card and the courage to be true to himself. I grew up and began my healing journey. This was the ultimate test of trust in God.

The next time I went into the office to work, I found myself talking to one of the attorneys.

"I need to get a divorce. Can you educate me on the process and procedures involved?"

In less than fifteen minutes, she had not only educated me about my options but had gotten all the information she needed from me.

"The sooner you get him to sign this, the sooner I can file your petition." She said, the next time we talked.

The lawyers at Sanctuary for Families had no problem stepping in. Six months later, I was divorced.

From that moment, the end of my life with Cesar and my relationship with the Creator became clearer. Intermittently I felt pain and missed Cesar. I thought about the dreams we dreamt and felt the sadness. Then I remembered my connection to the Great Spirit/Creator. That is where I found comfort.

As a child, I remember praying to God for the things that I wanted and getting disappointed when they were not granted. Of course, I would never get too angry with God for fear of being punished. God being a punishing God was an old tape I had to get rid of. I sometimes wondered if I was undeserving. Then I realized that praying for God's will was safer, less risky. It was more comforting to know that whatever happened in my life was purposeful. God was in charge.

After the divorce, I realized I had the ultimate say on how things turned out in my life. I can ask for what I want, need, and desire without the fear of disappointment or the compulsion of attachments. My goals are sometimes achieved and sometimes not. That I can still trust God and all its many representations, is miraculous. It is my faith that presents me with the opportunity to stretch beyond the moment and return to my highest self, my God self.

My old life was hard, challenging, unfair, cold, and lonely. But deep in my heart, when I thought about the regrets, I could not help but think of how far I had come. The experiences and decisions I regretted were the ones responsible for who I became.

I reflected on my regrets and found profound truths in each of them. For example, I regretted my parent's separation but the truth is, they had been apart for many years prior to their separation. I regretted running away from my mother's home when I was thirteen but that path ultimately led me to freedom. I could certainly say I regret staying up late, drinking with my brother-in-law, trying to fit in and get attention. But that horrific experience allows me to relate to the people I serve through my practice.

I deeply regret sending my brother away when he came to me seeking help. Through that experience, I learned that even when you love someone, you cannot always save them. I also regretted some of the choices I made or the ones that were made for me. I try to focus on the good that came from the pain of those choices. Do

I wish my life had been easier? Absolutely. But I have no regrets for what touched me and molded me into who I am today.

I waited for the permission to be free for many years not realizing I had been released from that bondage long ago. My self-blame and judgment were my own imprisonment. The confinement of cold, iron bars that I placed around my heart.

Not allowing myself to play, rest and laugh or honor the life I earned and deserved. Not loving myself but hoping for someone other than self to find me worthy of love. I have since concluded that to regret any aspect of my history is to regret aspects of myself. Today, when presented with the question, do I have any regrets, it is with great relief and joy that I can say no. I accept all of who I am. I am at peace with myself.

I can reflect, understand, and accept who I have been. I am free of blame and judgment. I honor, love, and respect my journey as it continues to develop. Life has blessed me with all that I need. I am reaping the reward of struggles, the quiet peacefulness of awakening. I am eager to get on my knees and express gratitude.

I remember seeing the reflection of the woman I had become from the corner of my eye. I saw her eagle eyes and wondered if she could see me. I hoped, prayed, and knew her time was close. I could feel the warmth and excitement of great potential. I was pregnant with joyful expectations. Soon darling, soon! The wind had picked up and she was on her way. Soon darling...

Divine Mother feeds me, feeds that child that has waited to be fed. Fed not by any mother, but by my mother. The beautiful, peaceful, nurturing, loving, passionate, strong, wise, playful mother. The mother I had yearned for. The mother that grew within me.

13
Letting the Future Unfold

A couple of years after I graduated from social work school, I was offered the position of Director of Counseling at Sanctuary for Families. I was excited and looked forward with great anticipation to what the future held. I was grateful and, later, in awe of how my life continued developing and unfolding.

No doubt, I had learned a lot in Social Work school. I learned more about myself and the challenges and issues of individuals, the complexities of societies, realities of oppression, and misuse of organizational and political power. I also learned about the systems created to maintain the status quo. I did not however, learn much about the different aspects of healing and how to access true wellness.

Periodic visits to Kripalu watered the seeds of faith I planted through my healing work. There were times when I closed my eyes and could imagine the unique smell of the space at Kripalu, a combination of Nag Champa incense and lavender oil. My mind would immediately quiet down, and my heart was filled with comfort. Although I was far from my real home, I felt like I had arrived at a second home. It is there I would learn what being home was really like. That home is unique and personal to everyone; that home is within our very own physical body and heart.

Prior to my visits to Kripalu, I struggled with accepting my body and being at peace with it. My body was not always a safe and peaceful place to arrive at. Slowly I came to appreciate and accept my body. It had not betrayed me; the people in my life betrayed me. My body allowed me to survive. I came to understand that my body is mine to inhabit, rest in and marvel over.

On every trip to Kripalu, I would stop at the bookstore and gift shop after settling into my room. I would unpack and sit for a moment of gratitude and meditation. At the dorms, I wondered what my five roommates would be like. I was always glad and relieved to be one of the first to arrive. By getting there early, I got to claim the top bunk closest to the door, where I could make sure to see everything.

The gift shop had books on meditation, conscious living, Yoga, affirmations, essential oils, massage therapy, Reiki, and many other things I wanted to learn about. They had the most beautiful crystals, amethyst, rose quartz, smoky quartz, citrine, and hematite, to name a few. They had chanting music, which I loved, and incense, clothing, postcards, inspirational journals, and much more. All of this contributed to the atmosphere of conscious living and peace.

It was at Kripalu that I experienced my first therapeutic massage. What an experience that was. I was excited and scared at the same time.

I had read that a therapeutic massage could help you relax, de-stress, detox, and improve your circulation. It sounded great, or so I thought. What about being naked and having someone you do not know see and touch your body? I remember wondering if I would be safe and able to relax? Filled with anticipation and no expectation, I decided to trust the process. I had learned not to let fear paralyze me. I could live on the edges of my life, or I could jump into the center, take risks, feel the fear, and do things anyway.

Yes, it was a bit weird to disrobe, including my underwear, and slip under the sheet, face down. I remember thinking, why my underwear? Then I decided to keep my panties on. For me, it was bad enough to be behind closed doors.

But it was mostly wonderful. It felt good to be touched the first time for the purpose of healing. I was being touched by someone whose primary purpose was to offer me loving, respectful, and unconditional comfort. As much as I worried about her crossing the line, I eventually realized she would not and did not. This would be one of many massage therapy sessions I had. It was always such a sacred and beautiful experience. The soft meditative music and pretty smells. The therapist's gentle but firm touch and respectful demeanor. Her focus and spirit of service made for a magically restorative experience. I have had the best sleep on the massage table, the deepest cries, and experienced the most acceptance I ever encountered – and from a stranger.

I soon came to understand that therapeutic massages were indeed healing. They offered many physical benefits. What came as a surprise was the emotional and psychological impact of doing massage therapy and energy work. Through massages, my body released emotions I didn't know were still there. Yes, the body does hold memories, good, bad, and indifferent. When we surrender and allow ourselves to face our fears, the body can let go of years of sadness, grief, and shame. Often, there is also anger to be released. This was my experience and that of many people I've had the honor of serving.

I remember inviting a client at Sanctuary for Families to allow her wounds to speak. I guided her to simply place her hand over her bruised eye and let the words flow. It was such a powerful experience for her and me as a witness. The body remembers what we do not and waits for the opportunity to express itself. I would become committed to offering others the chance to heal through massage therapy. I provided what I then called psycho-therapeutic massages. These sessions were an opportunity to verbally express and process thoughts, memories, and sensations that came up through the massage experience.

At Kripalu, I also got the opportunity to explore aromatic essential oils extracted and distilled from the essence of medicinal plants. I used a concoction of essential oils I came up with to address my depression and anxiety.

It was a mix of geranium and lavender oils or sometimes peppermint and lemongrass I used to give me energy and help me focus.

The gift and bookstore at Kripalu had things that probably saved my life. And in retrospect, I see how it prepared me for so much more than social work school ever could.

When I reflect on these periods of my life, I realize I often felt like I was just going along. A friend once said to me, "Girl, you are really wiser than you let on."

I had no idea what she was talking about. She was one of those friends whose opinion I honored. She was considered an elder not just in age but certainly in wisdom. When I'd ask her a question about something I thought I knew nothing about, she would say, "Girl, you know!"

The first time she responded that way, I thought she was joking. She was not.

"Come on. Tell me how I am supposed to know? I have no idea what you are talking about. Why would I pretend not to know?" I would say.

She would look me straight in the eyes and tell me again, "Girl, you know!"

She clearly saw in me something that neither of us could understand. She saw something in my inner being. I would come to understand what she saw in me. I did, in fact, know things. I did not know how I knew, but I did. It was like I had an internal guide. I could always see a storyline forming and developing. I had been gifted with the ability to discern when to follow along.

There are probably thousands of times I could have gotten into lots of trouble. For the most part, my going along has been quite divine. But the times I failed to follow my intuition; things did not go so well.

I went into social services because a friend suggested it. I volunteered because someone else was doing it. I got involved with Yoga, 12 step programs, and even Social Work graduate school because I was going along. I have come to understand that my going along was me being open to inner guidance. Life presented me with opportunities that I did not question. I thought I was blindly trusting and that mostly, I had gotten lucky. I knew somewhere in my deepest wisdom that things were going to work themselves out. I knew that the next right thing, the next necessary step, would be made clear to me. I kept saying yes to life, and life kept saying yes to me.

The way my life was unfolding was not random. Yes, I had been going along. But, I did so because of a strong desire to be good and do good, as my spiritual teacher, Guru Satchidananda, would often tell us. I did not know why but it had become important to me to be just, ethical, and loving. I thought it had something to do with my experiences which were all contrary to who I wanted to be. I was determined to have a decent life.

I was driven to continue saying yes to life; however, it came to me. And life just kept revealing and presenting me with experiences that I went along with.

I was also determined to understand what had happened in my family. Why was there so much turmoil? Why the hardship and dysfunction? What decided some of us making it and others not? Ever-so-often, I thought about a story I heard repeated by my family members many times. I never heard it firsthand from the woman it revolved around, but boy, was it popular. It seemed like everybody—Mom, Dad, my siblings, and even some family friends, recalled it and loved to emphasize the punch line.

"The Molina family will pay for what they did to me."

That line would pop into my thoughts. Particularly when I was scared or felt bad for myself or could not explain something strange that had occurred. It was then that I would hear someone say, "Hertrudis cursed us."

Hertrudis was a woman whose heart, my father and brother, broke. The rumor was, she was not going down as just one more victim of the Molina's. One day, angry, frustrated, and ashamed, she stormed out, saying, "The Molinas will pay for what they have done to me. I swear on my dead body, they will pay for it."

That incident is what made me wonder if the Molinas were cursed? Did I defy the curse, or was I not a true Molina? Or perhaps they—my sister, brothers, and parents—did not resist enough? Was I exempted? And if so, why?

Some people say that believing in curses is immature and that uneducated people or kids spend time worrying about it.

"We make what we make of our lives! That black magic thing is for weak-minded individuals and devil worshippers," is what people said.

It was another common belief to argue the validity of curses. But at times, I wondered if it was possible to be wished evil and have it affect your life and the lives of those around you. I wondered if it could even affect the lives of unborn generations.

There was a time I believed my family was cursed. I toyed with the reality that there were just too many odd occurrences in my family for it to be anything other than a curse. When I think about how, when, and where most of the Molinas left the earth, died, the validity of curses seems believable. My father was the first to go. After my mother left him for a woman, he was heartbroken. He never gave up or let go. He had always been reluctant to see doctors. Still, He agreed to go into the hospital for a triple bypass heart surgery.

He was convinced it would make him strong enough to win his wife back. The surgery was a success, but he coughed himself into severe hemorrhaging post-surgery, which ultimately killed him in his late 60's.

My 30-year-old brother, Daniel's body, was found mutilated in a black garbage bag in an open lot in Spanish Harlem. Police asked my poor mother to identify him by the cap he always wore. He was only twenty-seven and had no children. The last time I saw him was when he came to me asking if I would keep my mother because he was in danger. Some believe it was Carlos, Lucy's husband, who put a hit on him. Daniel had been one of his drug dealers.

Then my brother Luis died of natural causes at the age of 46 after having lived most of his adult life with mental illness and homelessness. I swear, as sad as it was to see him go, particularly because it broke my mother's already-broken heart, I was happy for him. His suffering was finally over. He was another Molina who had no children.

Then my older sister Lucy's two children passed away. One at fourteen and the other at twenty-five. Lucy had to bury them both, one before and one after she buried her husband, Carlos.

My cute baby niece Lisa went first. How does a fourteen-year-old die of complications of obesity? She was close to three-hundred pounds, and I often wondered if her father got to her as well. Had she taken my place when I left? What did they do to her when I left, running for my life?

My nephew Andy died of a massive heart attack at age twenty-five. He was also morbidly obese. They were both so sweet. After running from their home, I never saw them again. I did not go to either of their funerals. For me, they had died the day I left.

And then Carlos died. He had caused more than enough damage for one lifetime. I am not sure how he left, and I never asked. But I know he died after living in a wheelchair due to having a stroke. I saw him once during a rare visit to their home. I felt a mix of disgust and pity for him, but mostly I felt indifference. He sat in a wheelchair, unable to speak. He appeared to be paralyzed. I remember wondering how much he had suffered and if it was at least a fraction of the suffering he caused others.

I felt relief, I knew he would never abuse a child again.

They say the most devastating thing for a mother is to bury her children. That was an experience both my sister and mother shared. I guess neither of their hearts could endure it. First, my mom died of complications of diabetes. Not able to process sweetness, that was my metaphysical definition of diabetes. Mom departed shortly after my brother Luis left. I will always believe she died of heartbreak—misery and not enough sweetness.

Then my sister Lucy left. I am uncertain what she died from, but I can tell you that she, too, was morbidly obese and could have died of diabetic complications or heart failure. She also could have died from pure loneliness, shame, and guilt. She was only 56.

Lucy never accepted responsibility for abusing me, even after I gave her the chance to ask for forgiveness. She came close to accepting that her husband abused me. Lucy felt she, too, was a victim, and she probably was. But unlike her, who could defend herself, I was a defenseless child.

The odd thing is not so much that all those Molinas left, but that those associated with the offspring of my mother and father and their offspring were gone too. Of all the Molina children, only three were left. Thankfully, my sister Zulema had children. I have two nephews. As much as Antonio and I both love kids, neither of us ever had children.

I do not deny that Hertrudis probably did wish people in my family pain and discontent. Hurt people, hurt people. But I do believe a curse is only as powerful as your belief in it is.

The conscious or unconscious belief in the power of a so-called curse kept the focus of the Molina's and their consequential experiences on something or someone other than themselves. I vowed to be mindful of what I believed and told myself. I believed in the laws of karma, cause, and effect, reaping what you sow and, most importantly, the Creator. I vowed to believe that only we can curse ourselves if we give power to negative beliefs.

The Molina curse was probably the result of us standing in our own way and reinforcing negative beliefs in our thoughts. I had broken that supposed curse by saying yes to life and the Creator, no matter what.

I wanted to be authentic, to be in a safe environment, and live life to its fullest. I wanted respect, which meant I had to respect others. I also wanted to be guided, taught, and led to good places. I took life on with the determination to be and feel empowered. Taking life on led me to make decisions and choices that would teach me important things about myself.

I also wanted to see all of me, the good and the bad. That meant being honest with myself and others. I gravitated towards doing service, helping, and loving others. It was not an Eros love but an Agape type of love that was pure, genuine, and without attachments or expectations. I believed everyone was entitled to feel loved. This attitude motivated me and grew something new in me that I have come to know as energy and spirit. It was this energy that kept me moving toward goodness. This was also the energy that drove the engine and allowed me to go along with the unfolding of my purpose.

I learned to follow my purpose instead of the negative energy of a family who believed they had been cursed. These lessons would later serve me in my professional work and on my journey.

The knowledge I gained at my first few jobs confirmed that what I had experienced at the hands of my sister and her husband was abusive. I had done nothing to bring that on myself. There was nothing any child could ever do to warrant being manipulated and forced to do things they could not legally consent to. The domestic violence my sisters and mother experienced was also an unfortunate reality. Sadly, these incidents were much more prevalent in our society than I ever imagined.

In graduate school I learned about my family. I came to understand that for me to help others, I first had to help myself, then I could be deeply compassionate, and understanding of another's pain.

I would also come to understand the resiliency of human beings. My childhood and adolescent experiences prepared me to fulfill my work and purpose. I wished I had not gone through the horrific experiences of my childhood. But, there was good that came out of the pain.

I embarked on a journey toward wholeness. I searched for healing and allowed myself to be helped and supported. I showed up open and honest. I trusted and believed in the process. I learned that within me lived a young child who needed guidance. That child stopped growing when she was being abused and needed discipline and structure. What she needed and yearned for the most was love and acceptance. Through my healing journey, I accepted the job of watching over that little girl. I learned to talk to her and ensure she had whatever support she needed. This was only the beginning.

In time, it all came together. My friend was right. I did know something. I was not fully aware of what I knew, but it would be crystal clear one day. I knew then about spirit, resiliency, trust, and faith in something greater than myself. I learned about hope, love, and compassion. I knew about being of service. I knew about purpose and willingness. I knew I was ready to live my purpose.

I also knew about healing and supporting others to do the same. I learned and came to master human behavior, development, and psychodynamics. I was taught counseling techniques and measurable models. I dedicated myself to non-traditional learning, which gave me the foundation for the more significant work I would do.

My life experiences provided me with something unteachable. I have often been asked to explain what I do with clients. Other therapists wanted me to explain how I learned to do the interventions I did and how I knew to say and or do what I did.

There were many aspects of my intervention style I could share and teach. But some of my gifts had developed because of my personal experience. I am grateful to be of service to the clients I serve. I see their hearts and pain. Because of what I went through, I can provide them with a sense of hope. I can testify that things get better if they do not give up.

I join them, not in their pathology but as human beings. I see them as my siblings. I join them in the way I have wanted others to join me. I see them with respect and honor their process.

I have always known that we are all one. I found myself saying this to clients. When a client heals, it heals a part of me and others in the group. This is one of the meanings of being all one.

I share my gratitude with my clients for their commitment to healing themselves. I also explain that they are not only healing their lives, but when they commit to healing themselves, they heal past and future generations. They experience my heart, my caring, and my dedication to their wellbeing. Some of them trust me more than they have allowed themselves to trust anyone. At the end of the day, I believe we're all seeking to be seen and loved. My job is to create spaces in people's lives where this can happen. I share my story to help open them to an idea, reflection, or vulnerable place in their experience. When I see someone surrendering to a place of hope, it is confirmation that I know what I know.

When I am sitting with someone who has lost hope and feels relieved and hopeful within the course of our time together, I know I am divinely guided. I remember working with a young man who was all talked out. I asked him if he wanted to receive an energetic healing medicine called Reiki while we spoke. As I worked on him, he expressed his desperation and loneliness. The longer we sat together, the less he spoke. I could see him relaxing and letting go. I could see him going to a place where he felt safe. After the session was over, he said he felt much better.

"I felt like I was back home," he told me. He referred to being back home in his country of origin with his grandmother, who loved him. He asked if we could do a Reiki session again. It's moments like these I feel so incredibly grateful to be fulfilling my purpose.

I had been preparing or was being prepared to step into a place where I could consciously follow my purpose. I understood why I was put on the planet. I was a healer. Ever since I got in touch with this realization, that is the work I have been doing. Helping others heal and return to a place of wholeness and holding space for them to step into their authenticity, their true self, with love and light.

To be enlightened means "To be educated, informed and lettered. To be literate, aware, liberal, and sophisticated. To be refined, cultivated, open-minded, knowledgeable, and broad-minded."

To these terms, I add the word teachable. For me, it has been a process of learning, relearning, and most of all, remembering to reclaim what I have always known. I used to feel fearful of the memories. I had been forced and convinced to forget what I knew. When I claimed my knowledge of self, I understood what it meant to be teachable. Obviously, it is important to know what you know, but it is also essential to know that there's always room to learn more no matter how much you know. To be further informed, educated, cultivated, and self-aware.

I have come to know how true it is that teachers are everywhere. I realized there are teachings in the trees, the skies, animals, and all situations. The question is, can I recognize that I am being taught even when I do not recognize the lessons. Am I taking note of the teachable moments that are being created, consciously and unconsciously, moments that move me toward my wholeness and greatness? As a student, I have learned to listen for and seek lessons with all my senses.

I have always been opened to discovering new teachers. Once I found them, I would move into the receiving place with a willingness to embrace their offerings. We are all simultaneously teachers and students. It is a gift to know a teacher who does not exploit or manipulate and is not arrogant—a teacher who allows themselves to be taught. Occasionally I ask myself, what have I learned from my surroundings and my life?

My mother was one of my greatest teachers. Making peace with and learning to respect my mother was one of my most important lessons. I came to understand generational and intra-generational trauma and how dysfunction can be passed down in the form of traditions and learned behaviors.

I could not appreciate all she taught me when I was full of hurt and resentment. I resented her for not being present, for always being too sad and depressed to care for my siblings and me. I came to understand that my mother had done the best she could do. She had been suffering for a long time, way before I was born. By the time I came into the family, my mother had given birth to nine children. She had miscarried a couple of times at an advanced stage and even had a child die at birth. She suffered emotional and physical abuse from my father. It was not always clear who was the abuser and who was being abused. What was clear was that my father's family values were not above board. He thought having affairs was part of being a Latin man.

My father thought being a provider was how a man earned honor. My mother was his second marriage or long-term relationship. Theirs had been my mother's first marriage.

From my relationship with my mother, I learned compassion and forgiveness. I came to respect her for all she had endured, as well as her resiliency and strong spirit. She died at the age of sixty-six. She was still a fighter.

Before she died, she still had not figured out what God's purpose for her life was and why He had not taken her yet. She tried hard to find joy and peace. She finally came to a place where she accepted her life, and I came to a place where I could accept her. She did the best she could with the cards she was dealt. She was my mother.

Although we did not talk much about her childhood, I have this memory, or perhaps it is just my narrative, that she had grown up in a Catholic convent. Like her eldest son, she had one sibling who was homeless and suffered some undiagnosed mental illness.

The more I accepted my mother, the more I let go of the shame and guilt about the things I had been through. I realized that I, too, had fallen into the role of a helpless, dependent victim. I had to learn how to set limits and boundaries, how to say no, and when I needed to walk away. I had to learn it was okay for me to be happy and have a good life, even if people around me—particularly my mother—did not have that.

This realization began a relationship with what would become an even greater teacher. My healing journey. Little did I know that my early childhood experiences would be the most complex and most productive lessons I would have. Because of those early lessons, I am the teacher and student I am today. The need to understand and heal my wounds led me to a search to find the pieces that would make me whole again.

It began with seeing a traditional therapist who could help me see myself. She gave me the wisdom that I was responsible for my journey. It was during this time that I discovered the importance of movement. My visits to Kripalu availed me the opportunity to explore my emotions and express them through movement, particularly dance and Yoga.

By observing my body, I learned that memories could elicit emotion. Instead of acting on or reacting to the emotion or resorting to an impulsive response, I could pause and process the feelings. I tuned into how my body felt. To my surprise, usually, my body wanted to move without restrictions. At first, I did not understand how it all worked. But I have come to realize that the nervous system holds the charge of our memories. When given time and space to heal itself, the body knows what it needs. I would go to any length to allow myself to participate in a movement and dance healing experience.

After a long day of work, I would prepare to take the journey up north to New Jersey. I deeply looked forward to being away and having time to focus on taking care of myself.

I packed the car with all my comforts, ready for my four-hour journey. Despite the heavy traffic and the stormy weather, everything was going well. When I got close to my exit off the New Jersey Turnpike, my obsession began. Every five minutes, I checked the directions I had printed from MapQuest. My anxiety built to the point of my inability to retain the directions written on the paper. I talked out loud to myself while driving.

"What's the exit number? I cannot make a mistake and get lost. Shit. Relax. Do not panic, or you'll start feeling out of control. Stop it! You're self-doubting again."

Finally, thank God, I would see the exit. As I exited the freeway, I got a moment of relief. One part of the journey was completed. But the rain was still pouring down. The sky was black, and the streets were not brightly lit. Obsessively, I continued to look at my directions. Then my worst nightmare happened.

"Oh no, I have to go."

I had an incredible urge to go to the bathroom and relieve my bladder. I saw myself as if I were watching someone else. I was in a state of complete anxiety. I was hungry. After all, I would not stop to pick up something to eat because I didn't want to lose any time.

The moment of triumph and comfort I experienced getting to the NJ Turnpike had dissolved. Nothing made sense, and there was no one around to assist. I wondered what I was doing in New Jersey, looking for Bloomfield Community College. I'd made a big mistake. My bladder was about to burst, and my time was running out. Filled with frustration, tears running down my face, I pulled over. I asked myself again, what the hell are you doing here?

For one short moment that felt like an eternity, I was reminded of my pain, frustration, fear, and anger. The memory of all those who had abandoned, abused, raped, and made empty promises to me came pouring in. I felt like a motherless child, alone and helpless. It was as if a black cloudy sky had fallen over me. All I could think about was how helpless and alone I felt. I was unable to remember my faith or escape the horrible feeling in the pit of my stomach. I felt like a vulnerable child who wanted to go back home where it was safe, warm, and dry. I forgot that God had brought me all the way from Maryland, four hours from home, and years away from my trauma. It dawned on me to ask why I would be abandoned now?

I managed to pull a towel from my bag on the back seat and relieve myself. As the warm, wet urine poured out of me, I let go of the shame and surrendered. Lord, did I feel pitiful.

This was the point I usually gave up on. I would accept I had no power to fight the Big Bad Wolves (perpetrators). I would lay there, swallow my tears, eat my pride, and focus on the ceiling (disassociated). I would tell myself it was not so bad and that it would pass.

If I could let go of a moment of horrible dread and humiliation, life would get easier. That moment would pass away into the place of memories of them FUCKING WITH ME. It was then I realized no one was fucking with me anymore. No one had fucked with me in a long time.

And the voice within said, "It is okay, sweetie. Don't be scared, don't be ashamed, and don't give up. You deserve to be here. No one is ever going to fuck with you again. You are only lost in New Jersey. You are a little wet, tired, and hungry, but you will be okay. You'll arrive later than you thought but so what. You'll be fine. No one will judge or punish you, and if they did, does it matter? Do they know where you've been? They'll understand that you drove all the way from Maryland. Just as you arrived, you took a detour back to the '70s to Brooklyn, New York, where you learned to fight for your life. You chose life and fought yourself back to Jersey."

I had only needed to talk to the scared little girl within. It was up to me to comfort her, hold her and calm her down. From then on, I chose to be present for my new life. I chose to be powerful. I chose to be a survivor. There was a relief of that moment coming to closure. The black cloud had passed. I drove to the next corner and looked up. I took a deep breath and chuckled. I had arrived at my destination.

Years later, I still have those moments—each time I choose the survivor in me. I retrieve my soul, my true self. Each time I go through the healing process, I return to my body sooner. I am always so incredibly grateful.

As I pulled into the parking lot and exited the car, I knew it was going to be a wonderful weekend. It already was. I entered the space present, aware and ready to be taught. As soon as I walked into the building, my belly pulsed, and my body felt warm. I was committed to speaking the truth, looking into people's eyes, and seeing the openness.

I honored my attraction for a woman's body without shame, without being repulsed by my desire to look, to appreciate beauty for beauty itself. I recognized myself in the women in the room. Beautiful, strong, and deserving. When my heart settled down, when my pulse slowed, I knew I had transformed the pity and shame and chosen myself. The student had arrived.

There was a room full of teachers there that day. I was given another opportunity to work on the muscles of receiving and accepting. Spirit had blessed me with the opportunity to strengthen, reprogram and return to myself. To choose growth and nurture the truth.

I was invited to the dressing room to change into my dance clothes and go to the studio. I thanked the spirit. It is almost like it knew I needed to change my pissy, wet clothes.

I walked into the studio feeling alone and scared. The old programming took over again. My opportunity for growth almost turned into a bout of self-pity.

Almost.

I walked into a room full of women. Music was playing. The women were moving around, dancing, and engaging with each other. I quickly dropped off my bags and joined them. I connected with the first woman who noticed me. Later, she would tell me that she had zeroed in on my strong, wise, open stature. I was open even though I felt closed, small, and pitiful. She immediately touched my heart and proceeded to welcome me into hers. It was like two warriors meeting, both willing to be seen. We were vulnerable, asking for help, exhausted, and wanting to be fed.

The facilitator spoke of being at the well and taking notice when you are thirsty. She encouraged us to go to the well and drink. To let ourselves move and dance as if we were the lead dancer in a Broadway show, to follow the rhythm of our breath and heartbeat. To stop and go whenever we wished.

We moved as if each of us were lead dancers. We let the cello, harps, drums, and each other's energy feed and nurture us.

I quickly stepped onto the stage, my stage. I liked the feeling of being at the well, the fountain of life, and permitting myself to drink from it. I drank abundantly. I drank until the water poured out of me and became me. I became one with all that I am. It felt like the thirst would never be quenched. I wanted to drink as much as I wanted, for as long as I needed, until the water and I became one.

I noticed the other woman again. She was strong and grounded like a mountain. Just as I opened myself to receiving her, I noticed she was reflecting on another part of me. I looked into her eyes and saw more of myself. Her gentle, independent gaze revealed she was present without asking for anything in return. She was safe and consistent.

For a moment, I was taken aback. I caught my breath. Then I had an epiphany. I was being offered sustenance by another woman.

She chose to feed me. She loved me because she felt my hunger. Respectfully, appropriately, honoring herself and me. The boundaries were clear. Again, she offered her spirit to me without expecting anything in return.

The race was coming closer to an end. I wanted to be caught. I wanted to be sat down and made to slow down. Every ounce of my body was screaming; please hold me. Hug and shower me with your love and attention. See me and ask nothing in return. Just that I receive. Receive me just the way I am.

I could choose to receive, give me back to myself, and give myself the gift of rest, joy, play, and excitement. I could continue the cycle or start a new cycle.

There was no one to blame. I was free to drink from the well until my cup runneth over. I was free to skip in the rain, roll down the hill and be silly. I was free to be still, strong, generous, loving, and caring.

An open heart can give and receive. An open heart allows us to stay present in our bodies, aware of our thoughts and feelings. I chose to be who I am, deserving. At the thought of being me, my heart pounded, then settled down, my pulse slowed.

As I stayed present in my body, I heard a voice say, "I invite you to play, laugh, and choose you, as you. Truly you. Not who they want you to be."

I heard the music and saw all the women. I saw them and saw me. Every one of us was powerfully stepping into our lives.

After about forty-five minutes of dancing and moving, we were encouraged to slow down our movement and gently bring it to a stop. I can still feel my breath settling down and my heart rate returning to a normal pulse. For the next half hour, we journaled about our experience.

The facilitator told us, "There is no need to question, analyze or judge the experiences you had. Just write whatever comes to you."

14

Learning to Live with Loss

Two years after my divorce from Cesar was finalized, I embarked on casual dating. I had gone out on exactly two dates. I did not feel a connection to either of the guys I went out with. If I were to open myself up to another relationship, I wanted someone healthy. I was not going to conjure this man on my own. I asked Creator to help me manifest this person. I wrote Great Spirit a letter asking for a new partner. This person needed to be someone who would love and understand me and support my continuing to uncover who I was. Maybe it would be someone in the process of finding themselves or who was no longer searching.

My letter said: Dear Great Spirit, I thank you for my life and the many gifts, miracles, and wonderful experiences you have allowed me. Thank you for guiding me through the darkness and pain. I trust in you and believe that you and only you, almighty Creator of all, can now bring to me a person I can share the rest of my life with. I trust that whomever you send me will be the right person. I trust in you.

And as I paused, thinking that my letter was done, I had the impulse to share a few more details of who I wanted. I understood that Creator did not need my help, and I laughed at the thought. Still, I thought it would not hurt. And so, I added:

May they be caring, patient and compassionate, family-oriented, and responsible. May they be educated and professional, driven, and a person of faith with an awareness of the difference between spirituality and religion. May they be good-looking, tall, and strong.

I also heard myself say, "And you know God, how about an African-American. I'm ready for something different."

One day at school, as I walked down the hall, I noticed a meeting in the auditorium. I never seemed to make time for events like this. But this day, for whatever reason, I became intrigued. Nicole, a tall, beautiful African American woman I had seen before, stood speaking. We had run into each other near the elevators at Hunter Social Work School and said hello. She seemed like a pleasant enough person. But on this day, when I entered the auditorium, something registered with me. I truly saw her. There she was, standing at the podium, talking about gay and lesbian rights, and advocating on their behalf. She was gutsy, and I have to say, I was impressed.

Ours was friendship at first sight. Nicole's ambition, determination, and commitment to justice and human rights were what I liked most about her. We became very close friends. So close that after graduating college, Nicole and I went into a shared private practice. That was where we really got to know each other.

During one of the most challenging times of my adult life, Nicole was right there to support me and offer encouragement. She was my lesbian friend that kept me politically correct. It was interesting to learn about the lesbian, gay, bi-sexual, and transgender community and issues of injustice and oppression.

We also discussed other types of inequalities, including racism. We talked about our life experiences and families and came to realize we had a lot in common. I found it comforting to have a friend who seemed to really care. We came to trust each other.

It was not easy to work a full-time job and maintain a part-time private psychotherapy practice. At the end of an exceptionally long week, Nicole and I decided to treat ourselves to dinner. We enjoyed eating good food. As we finished our meal, I accidentally slammed my knee against the wrought iron leg of the table.

"Oh man, that hurt!" I said, grabbing my knee.

Nicole answered, "I'd love to say something to you, but I'd hate for you to get offended."

"Don't worry about protecting my feelings. I can take care of myself." I told her, still focusing on my hurt knee.

"Tell me, what were you going to say," I said, encouraging her to reveal her secret.

After a bit of coaxing, she confessed, "I'd love to rub your knee for you and make it better."

It took me a minute to get what she was saying. Was it possible? Was Nicole hitting on me? Yep, she was! I had asked for a partner. Maybe I was being granted a whole new life.

The Disney movie Aladdin had just come out. Nicole and I went to see the movie, and both fell in love with the theme song that talks about it being a whole new world. Indeed, I was embarking on a whole new world. My friendship with the person who would one day become my soul mate was a co-creation between Creator and me. I had prayed for someone who would honor and love me for who I was, not for what and how I could provide. I wanted someone I could honor and love for who they were rather than what they could provide. I remembered praying for someone intelligent, caring, and powerful, someone who used those traits in the pursuit of serving others. I prayed for someone who respected the importance of self-growth and personal evolution, someone with a spiritual foundation. God granted me that person and so much more.

I never felt more loved, cared for, and honored. Not only were they committed to self-growth and personal evolvement, but they also encouraged me to reach for my highest potential. Their faith was strong and clear. There was no doubt that they were who I prayed for and who God wanted me to be with. My self-respect, love, and faith in Creator expanded, and I felt deep in my heart that it would continue to grow. We not only saw but experienced the Goddess in each other and worked hard at honoring it.

I came to understand my power and responsibility at manifesting what I want. I had to act as if I deserved it and visualize it as already here. The secret of manifestation is asking, trusting that it will be, visualizing and sensing deep in your body – all the way to your nervous system and knowing that it is so. And so it is, and so it was.

I found it difficult to fully comprehend that my whole life had changed over a relatively short period of time since Cesar and I had divorced. Often, I thought of it as a series of different lives. From a place where I thought I would never separate myself from the dysfunctionality of my family. To escaping the violent injustices of crazy, derailed people like Lucy and Carlos and then finding a friend and a stabilizing force in my marriage to Cesar, to losing him, and finally, finding myself.

I was in love with life and myself. I was following my heart and doing what made me happy instead of what made me safe. I chose to believe in love again.

15

The Highs and Lows

A few decades later, with a few businesses under our belt, furnishing and re-furnishing several homes, three commitment ceremonies, and the final legal wedding, I was in yet another new life. There were many incredible, magical, and challenging experiences. God's orchestration manifested an amazing symphony.

Like everything else in life, there were many highs and lows in my journey with Nicole. The life-changing, memorable moments were many. Nicole and I were big into rituals and ceremonies. Take, for example, the reason for not one but, later, four commitment ceremonies, a private one to honor ourselves and our ancestors, another to honor our spiritual community, and then sharing our love and commitment to each other with our family friends, and colleagues. Finally, and I do mean finally, the clearly overdue legal marriage license ceremony, just because we could.

Amber, one of Nicole best friends, a spiritual elder, and a mentor in our community, held space for the most significant of these experiences. Ecstatic that Nicole had found the love of her life and eager to know the woman who had swept Nicole away,

Amber had a great curiosity about us. Just as we did on many other days, the three of us sat around telling stories, laughing, and eating.

This day, as we chatted about our relationship, Amber felt called to suggest and invite us to a "Chanunpa Ceremony" a sacred pipe smoking ceremony." We were to pray for our relationship and truly get to know each other. We were ministered to and encouraged to invite the guidance of the Great Spirit and each of our ancestors. Amber prayed for us as we smoked the Chanunpa. We remained grateful for this ceremony and for the opportunity to release our prayers through the sacred tobacco smoke. It is believed that the smoke delivers one's prayers to Tunkashila and Wakan Tanka, the native and Lakota references for Creator God.

After several hours, it was confirmed that Nicole and I knew each other from another life. This was not our first time being together. In one lifetime, I was a man who went by the name Rodolfo Marquez. He was a Spaniard merchant with a dark life and a violent temperament. He hooked up with women in every town, but he knew where love lived. And that love was with Nicole.

Nicole and I felt like we knew each other in a deeply profound way. Our relationship was a continuation and opportunity to get it right. I guess, or Rodolfo was finally ready to settle down.

Amber probed, "How do you know you truly want to be together? How will this relationship be different than others you've had? Are you ready to be of service to each other? Do you know what your individual and collective dreams are?

Will you protect your relationship before everything and anything? Will you have children? How Many? Where will you live? What's your vision for getting old together?"

She kept asking us questions, and we had an answer for each one. Later, we would stay up many nights talking, sharing, and discussing these same questions and many others. There was no doubt we intended to be together for a long time.

It felt like that day was stopped in time, that it would never end. After much sharing, Amber sat with us and held sacred space. We prayed, poured libation to our ancestors, and had moments of quiet reflections. The ceremony was to end with our paying homage to our ancestors and the African Orisha, Yemoja. We headed out for Orchard Beach in the Bronx. Amber gathered her tobacco and sage and asked that we get flowers and fruit for our offerings to the deity represented by the ocean. She encouraged me to bring my red Congas drums I had bought some years ago with my brother Luis's final monies from the city.

The beach was quiet, the ocean still, and there was a cool mist on this fall day that welcomed us. The sound of the drums was carried by the gentle breeze and softened by the waves. Amber prayed over us, blessing our relationship, and giving thanks to our Ancestors for bringing us together.

Amber pointed to the ocean. "Go pay your respects and get your blessings."

In an altered state, filled with magic, I wondered how I got so lucky. Nicole and I walked into the water, hugging each other, and baptized our new relationship by immersing ourselves in the vast, salty water of the ocean. We were grateful to Yemoja and all our ancestors.

As we reappeared, walking backward out of the ocean so we wouldn't turn our backs on our ancestors or Yemoja, there was Amber, ready to welcome us as one. She took off her beautiful blue-green Indonesian shawl and wrapped us in it. Years later, this shawl remains one of our favorites. Amber often reminded us that no matter how many other ceremonies we had, she was the one to re-affirm our ancient romance and pronounce us soul mates forever.

She was and is correct! Nothing topped that day. Over the years, when things were particularly challenging, remembering the truth of her words kept us moving forward. The emergent memory that Nicole and I came back into each other's lives in this lifetime for a reason still holds. I believe it was to support and facilitate our soul's growth, a journey of liberation and healing.

One of the gifts Nicole and I gave to each other was a commitment to assisting in the manifestation of one another's heart's desire. Over time this has been both a trial and a reward. A poignant example was the idea of becoming parents.

By the time we committed ourselves to each other, Nicole had decided that she was done with raising children. She had already raised her niece, a lover's child, and taken care of many other children. On the other hand, not only did I want to raise a child, but I also wanted to be pregnant. To me, conceiving a child and procreating was one of the greatest honors of human beings. I wanted to know what it was like to have the spirit of God growing in me.

From the moment I mentioned it, Nicole was committed. "No problem. There are many ways to make that happen."

We reflected and joked about how we were constantly working on some project. This time the project was me getting pregnant. We dreamed about the day we would have children. After several discussions and explorations, we settled on the least complicated process. We were going to a sperm bank.

Excitedly, we selected a sperm donor, one we consciously identified as African American, intelligent, artistic, and with as many features like Nicole as possible. Heart and soul, we dug in. Whatever it took, beginning with the morning charting of body temperatures to determine ovulation times. We made trips to the sperm bank to pick up the specimen. They placed it in an oversized liquid nitrogen tank that was frozen until ready for use. Off we would go with our four-foot-tall tank in a yellow cab, sometimes from Midtown and other times from Jersey.

We would be sitting in the back seat with that tank between us, praying over it from the moment we picked it up to the moment we got home. Anyone watching would have thought we were carrying home our first newborn baby. We would put the tank on our altar, pray and meditate over it. Being big on visualization, with the Grace of God, we just knew that if we set our intentions, we could manifest what we wanted.

On the right day, we doubled our prayers until the day my menstrual cycle started and began all over again. In-between inseminations and menstrual cycles, for a year of tries, I was always pregnant, so we thought. The sweet dreams of being pregnant sustained me. I enjoyed the belly rubs and the talks about how this time it was working, even after only a day or two of being late on my cycle. The letdowns disappointed us and became more difficult each time, but we did not give up.

We went from using the old lesbian turkey baster trick—keeping the pelvis elevated for at least forty-five minutes and resting for the rest of the day—to getting the inseminations done by an OB/GYN doctor and taking fertility medication. During these times, we knew for sure we were having twins. We had names picked out, had written welcome letters to the babies, and had Godparents selected.

Finally, at the doctor's suggestion, we stopped trying.

"Perhaps you're trying too hard. I suggest you take a break for a few months and give your body a rest." the doctor said.

Despite our extensive financial investment and failed dream, it was worth trying. If I had any doubt about Nicole's love for me, which I did not, this sealed it. She wanted a child as much as I did because she knew how much I wanted it. Even though I never got pregnant, we remember this year as one of joy, magic, hope, faith, and love, and loss.

Then there came my opportunity to witness a daughter's love for her mother. This was another unexpected gift. Ultimately, I came to love my mother and respect her for who she was. But I did not fully know what loving your mother meant until I saw Nicole interacting with her mother.

Unlike me, Nicole had an excellent relationship with her mother. Although Nicole's mom lived in another state, they often spoke, maybe several times a week. Nicole was forever telling stories about her mother, mainly expressing how proud of her she was. Her mom, Mrs. Sarah, was very loving and caring towards us. Every winter, she sent us a traditional box of fresh citrus fruits from her garden in Florida.

By the time I met Mrs. Sarah—Nicole's mom, she had begun showing symptoms of Alzheimer's. As her disease progressed, it became clear that Nicole and I would probably end up taking care of her. When Nicole said she was ready to get her mother and bring her home, I was not surprised. Mrs. Sarah became Nicole's primary purpose. She cared for her as though she was her most precious responsibility. I never heard her complain about or begrudge the tremendously difficult task of caring for her mother. Mrs. Sarah lived with us and under our care for years. I grew to love her.

Mrs. Sarah bought laughter, joy, tenderness, and strength to our marriage. And in the spirit of giving each other what the other wants, Nicole would care for her mother until she made her transition. And I was going to support her. In retrospect, the interesting juxtaposition of birth and death experiences shared between Nicole, and I was powerful.

I particularly remember the times when Mrs. Sarah would decide to dress herself. In the spirit of being respectful to her mother and honoring her mama's dignity, Nicole would put out her clothes for her to dress. At least that was the hope.

"Mama, you can't wear all that stuff. Either wear pants or a skirt. If you have a blouse on, you cannot put a short sleeve tee-shirt over it. And you certainly can't wear two hats in this heat." She'd lovingly tell her mother.

She knew her mother did not understand or have the capacity to make those decisions. Still, she hung in there until Mrs. Sarah miraculously gave in, or I interceded.

"Leave her alone. Let her wear what she wants." I would say.

"She's wearing too much stuff. Too many colors and layers." Nicole would respond.

"She has autonomy. Why are you messing with her styling choices? I think she looks rather Bohemian." I would say, and we would laugh.

I recall when I decided we should let her wear whatever she wanted and have a photoshoot instead of fighting it. Years after she was gone, we would still look at those photos and reminisce. I often told Nicole she was lucky to have her mom and how I wished I had been more accepting of my mom when she was still around. By this point, my mother had long since been gone. Many a day, I wished I had loved her unconditionally for who she was, not just for who I needed and wanted her to be.

The gifts I got from Mrs. Sarah were immeasurable. I was also able to make up for some of the experiences I missed with my mother. I remain grateful to Nicole and Mrs. Sarah for the motherly love and healing.

From the very beginning of our relationship and throughout the early years we were together, Nicole and I undertook the work of manifesting another dream of ours. We wanted to open a healing center for women and children. We fantasized about traveling there from New York City with friends and families. They, too, would be excited about our dream.

Then we got down to the nuts and bolts and started taking preparatory steps. First, we had to acquire land. Friends from the Eastern Shore of Virginia shared about the opportunities for purchasing land there. Before we knew it, we commenced doing just that.

Nicole stayed in New York, held on to her job, and handled all the financial responsibilities. As the strong-bodied, young, invincible me, moved to the Eastern Shore.

As a ceremonial Sun Dancer, I was convinced I could do anything – I'll move to the Eastern Shore and begin to set things up. Nicole planned to join me within a year.

During the period of preparation, I had several transformational experiences. I am reminded of the first time I went to Sundance invited by Nicole as a guest and helper. I remember how much I so desperately wanted to dance. The idea of being in communion with God with little or no distraction was such a sweet thought. At the end of the Ceremony, I pledged to come back. It was in the second year that I earned the right to dance.

Throughout the year, I fasted, meditated, prayed, and performed the other necessary rituals. The year of the big move to our dreamland on the Eastern Shore of Virginia was my third-year dancing. I attended the ceremony alone. Nicole would remain in New York while I traveled to New Mexico, then to the Ashram in Buckingham, Virginia, before arriving at the Eastern Shore.

Going to Ceremony alone was a little nerve-racking, but I told myself that I might as well get used to being away from Nicole. Besides, New Mexico, where the Sundance was held, was like being in a village of best friends and close family members.

Nicole had introduced me to her spiritual community, a group of women led by a Lakota family that gathered every year in the desert to perform Sundance. It was one of the most significant ceremonies in their tradition. I was honored to be introduced to this very sacred and private Ceremony.

We came together for ten to twelve days every year. Over one hundred women would get to work after preparing the land by clearing out nature's yearly debris. We erected structures that would be used as kitchens, designated waste areas, isolated healing and rest areas used during the ceremony. We created a Sacred Arbor to conduct the actual Sundance Ceremony. While working, we would catch up on the happenings of the prior year.

Many of the women traveled from the West Coast, but many of us came from the East Coast and even from out of the country. The atmosphere was intoxicated with laughter, love, and sisterhood. Children were running all over the fields. We came together to pray for the Harvest and the Lakota people. We lifted prayers for our families, friends, communities, animals, oceans, other water sources, and our great mother, the Earth. We also prayed for all our relations.

For days, we participated in Inipi, the Lakota Sweat Lodge ceremony. A sweat lodge is a purification ritual that helped prepare us for Sundance. Everyone was an integral part of the Ceremony. Some made sure water was available for the sweat lodges, bathing, and cooking. Others oversaw the cooking and feeding the community three meals a day. Others took care of the waste.

Some watched over the sacred fire that burned continuously from the moment we set foot on the land until we left. Others were responsible for keeping the firewood coming. A crew took care of the dancers. They were called healers. There was also the society that sang and provided the drumbeat to which the dancers prayed. Finally, we would be ready for what brought us together every year, the commitment and need to pray.

Never had I experienced anything as powerful as that Ceremony. It was a great expression of faith, tradition, and culture. The Sundance community was richly steeped in all three. We trusted that by coming together to pray and selflessly giving of ourselves, we had a chance to save our sisters and brothers who were struggling. This would be my third of a four-year pledge to dance. The tradition was to come together to support the Sundancers. They gave four consecutive days of dancing which became the prayer to the Creator, Tunkashila / Wanka Tanka.

We fasted, observed silence, and remained in prayer and meditation during this time. For me, this was a tribute to the Creator, a gesture of my gratitude, the least I could do to say thank you, Mother, Father, God. Tunkashila, Wakan Tankan, thank you for my life. Sundance gave me so much more than I could ever give back.

The third year was one of the most spiritually, mystical, and intense times of my life. We were between the second and the third round of the dance, and we were sitting in the rest area. I was pretty wired up. I had gone out to the sacred tree to pray, as many did while at rest. The area around the tree got very crowded. An overbearing desire to smoke a cigar came over me. Occasionally, I would smoke a cigar in other ceremonies but never at Sundance. And certainly not while dancing.

At Sundance, we smoked Chanunpas. When the sacred tobacco was released in the Chanunpa, it would travel up to Tunkashila, taking with it the heartfelt prayers of the dancers and people. I would place the pipe stem over my heart and hold the bow in my left hand in a symbolic gesture to bring the earth and sky together. I aligned myself with the Creator in a simple yet profound way by saying, "Mother, Father, everything God," recognizing God in all different forms and us in each other. I showed respect and gratitude for Spirit's magnificence. I thanked the Creator for receiving our prayers. It was an honor to witness that God is everywhere and available to all people if we believe.

I left the tree and proceeded to the rest area. From there, I could see my fellow dancers and our Chief praying and crying. Unlike the others, I felt agitated and restless. I turned to my dance sister and asked for one of her Cuban cigars. She looked at me as if she saw a ghost.

"Who told you I have Cuban cigars?" she said.

I have no memory of the details. But the story goes that I kept insisting until she had one of the helpers, medicine healers, go to the campsite to get me a cigar. What occurred that day seemed unfathomable.

We had only danced two rounds on that day when Ceremony took a totally different turn. I do not remember the transition, but it felt like I had an extreme out-of-body experience. Some people told me that it was as though I was channeling the spirit of an African Orisha. My energy was akin to Obatala, who is known as the father of humanity, Creator of humans, and the one who oversees and manages the spiritual heads of children. I remember seeing my physical self-transform. My posture became that of an elderly person; my voice changed to that of an old man. Those attending told me that even my gestures changed. I smoked at least six cigars and blessed people by spitting Gin over them. That too seemed very unusual given that this was alcohol-free land.

I had asked for the Gin, and someone new to the ceremony who did not know the rules just happened to have a quart of Gin they bought as an offering. This was a common practice in African and Caribbean spiritual traditions, but not at Sundance.

For hours, until the sun rose, I provided reflections and messages to every woman with children on the land. I spoke about the neglect of the children in the effort to be involved with the Ceremony. I pleaded that they do not forget the children. I stressed that it was important to spiritually protect, feed, and be attentive to the children's needs. I, or rather the Orisha Obatala, had a message for the grandmother of our Ceremony, our Chief's mother, the Ceremonial Elder.

The next day, filled with shame and self-judgment, not understanding what happened the night before, I wanted to isolate myself and avoid all interactions. But at the Sundance, there was nowhere to hide. To my surprise, while I worked up enough courage to face the community, our Ceremony Chief had gathered the community to discuss and process the previous day's occurrences. Apparently, the message had been deemed accurate. For the rest of the day, at the Arbor during the ceremonial dance, we focused on the wellbeing of the children and their parents.

For years after, people referred to that year's Ceremony as the year Obatala showed up through Santa. I remained conflicted and wondered if I had made it all up. Had I just been seeking attention? Deep down in my heart, I knew I would never dishonor our Ceremony by creating such a distraction.

That year, I read several books on the Orishas. I also learned more about Obatala and African religions. I spoke to several Elders, and everything confirmed that there was no way even the most outstanding actress could have dreamed up what happened that night. During this time, I got in contact with my true spiritual heritage. I was a woman of the earth. I believed in one God. My God was omnipresent, omnipotent, the Alpha and the Omega, Creator of all, Mysterious, Magical, Kind, and Forgiving. God was also omniscient and knew everything.

I came to understand that because God is so awesome, all forms, ways, and roads for people to worship sprang from One Source. This reminded me of the many times I had seen my mother honoring and worshiping representations of God. The Orishas, deities, and saints. I recalled my mother talking about San Miquel, San Lazaro, Santa Barbara, San Antonio, and many others. I remembered the parties and ceremonies back on 84th Street that our Cuban neighbor would offer to the community, her neighbors, and the guests of honor, the Orishas. I remember my mother lighting candles and giving offerings. Still, she did so with shame and secrecy because she had been conditioned to be ashamed of her indigenous practices. By learning more about the Orisha, I understood the connection between faith and oppression.

African and other indigenous religions were demonized and ostracized by leaders of the Catholic faith and other Christian religious systems. It was a way to control and rip away the power and connection of people of color to their ancestral beliefs.

Like my mother, I had been ashamed and afraid to explore my African religious roots. But I could not imagine anything had a more significant impact than the Sundance Ceremony experience the year Obatala appeared through me.

Being at the Ashram for a month came close. For years, I had practiced Hatha Yoga, Meditation and Pranayama, yogic breathing practices. Yoga had saved my life and probably the lives of those around me. I was excited to share the medicine with others and looked forward to being a certified yoga teacher.

The Ashram was quiet, clean, simple, and beautiful. After the unpredictability of the Ceremony, I needed the structure the Ashram offered. Getting up at five-thirty in the morning became a habit. I can still hear the violin music played by Swami Matagi. Awakening to a symphony of angels was the perfect way to enter a new, auspicious day. Her soft, beautiful skin, white hair, and God-like expression always invited us to accept her support and encouragement. She was our Bhakti teacher, teaching us about devotion and being of service to others, as though we were serving God.

I would walk into morning yoga and meditation practice with the sky filled with stars overhead. As I completed my morning practice, the sun would break through the horizon, just in time to greet us. I remember looking up to the sky and feeling tears on my face. They were tears of amazement, gratitude, and awe. Bursting with anticipation, I was ready to unwrap the gift of a new phase of my life: another day.

I loved the ease and simplicity of Ashram living. I could quiet the noise and distractions of the outside world and inside my head, which allowed me to hear my heart. The day would unfold the same way every day—meals, lectures, instructions, and practice.

The weekends were open for us to hang out and rest between morning, noon, and evening yoga and meditation practices and our Seva. Seva was selfless volunteer work and service to the community. This was absolutely the best learning environment I had ever experienced. By the end of the month, I was a certified Integral Yoga teacher proficient in meditation, yoga Asanas or poses, yoga Sutras, principles and philosophy, and pranayama. I could efficiently conduct an entire ninety-minute yoga class in Sanskrit.

I was so fortunate to have had a previous opportunity to be at an Ashram for an extended period. The 1st time I went to an Ashram was several years before my 3rd year of the Sundance Ceremony. I always loved going to Kripalu. I had started to prepare for my move to the Eastern Shore of Virginia. Getting a certification in Massage Therapy was a must.

At Kripalu, I had one of the most significant revelations about the body and how it heals. Human anatomy was the foundation of the massage therapy program at Kripalu.

I had to learn how to support the body, mind, and spirit at retrieving and completing stories that can get trapped in our bodies and keep us stuck. A great deal of instruction and practice buoyed me up to do this work. I developed the capacity to listen to my intuition and follow the still small voice within. I was a natural.

It was an awesome responsibility to be entrusted with someone's body. My hands could hear the needs of the muscles, cells, and even the body's energy. I could sense the stories it held and how to make room for them.

An outpouring of love, compassion, and grace would move through me. It was a gift from the highest, purest healing source and was beyond my human potential. This made me realize I was only an instrument being used by the Creator.

I learned things about an individual's body that had never been revealed. All I had to do was get out of my head and let the Source use my hands and heart. At Kripalu, I honed my respect for the body's ability to hold traumatic memories and, when offered the right environment, to heal them. In class this day, I was partnered up with a male student. Many of the women preferred to work with other women, but I did not care. I enjoyed the firmer touch and found myself suspicious of the lighter touch.

"Okay, Santa, take your time and turn over when you're ready." My massage partner said.

I could feel the sheet lift off my body as he worked on his draping, making sure my naked body was not exposed while I turned onto my belly. I adjusted myself and took a few deep breaths. It felt good to get my back worked on. Between the fragrance of the essential oils and his strong, warm hands, my body relaxed. For a moment or two, I even dosed into a twilight sleep. The intensity of my heart pounding awakened me. In a flash, my body heated up like I was on fire. My whole body tensed, and I realized what was causing these feelings. He was massaging my lower back and buttocks.

A surge of horror came over me. I started to cry uncontrollably. I felt a searing pain deep inside me. I heard myself shouting, "No, no, no! Just stop!"

My partner stopped immediately. Through my sobbing, I hear him saying, "It is okay, Santa. It is okay. You are okay. You're safe."

He continued to repeat the words, "You're safe now. You're safe,"

My thoughts played like a horror movie with memories of being sodomized. I had forgotten that day, the day I thought I would die. I had never experienced such pain. The rage and anger pushed into me until I could not cry, plead, or pray anymore. I left my body and returned when it was over. Although I had forgotten, my body remembered.

That day, I found my voice and regained the courage to speak out. My healing around that inhumane trauma advanced to a deeper level. I now had support around me. My requests were being honored. This allowed me to release my body, mind, and spirit from that horrible memory. I was no longer trapped. I was finally safe.

After being at the Sundance Ceremony, everything I did had a different feel to it. I danced my prayer in a one-hundred and twenty-degree temperature under the hot desert sun. I had no food and little water for four days. When you are connected to the Creator, all your needs are met.

I was blessed with licensure as a Massage Therapist from Kripalu. It was not luck that helped me move forward. It was the drive to fulfill a calling to be of service, to provide healing opportunities to others, particularly women and children. I had a mission to obtain training and skills before moving to the Eastern Shore of Virginia. There, I would use myself as a symbol of hope, a living example of what is within us. We all have the potential to heal if we believe we can and follow our calling. Nothing, absolutely nothing happens by mistake or goes to waste.

The Universe continued to prepare me for my larger mission. At some points, I must have said, "Yes, I'll do it. Yes, I'll follow your lead." I continue to say yes to the Universe.

Nicole and I could hardly contain our excitement as we planned our very first trip to the Eastern Shore. Not even a year prior, a friend had told us about a location in the Eastern part of Virginia. She was excited to be the one to take us to the area where we would open our healing center. Finally, we would get to go down South and realize the possibilities of manifesting our dream. The realtor sent us information about the area along with places we might want to stay during our visit. Once there, we would talk more about our plans. We browsed through the local newspapers and penny savers the realtor had sent us. The area was filled with bed and breakfasts, but one that excited us both was a place owned by Irene and Carol. How lucky could we get? There was no question of where we would stay. We figured that Irene and Carol were either mother and daughter, sisters, or lovers. We told each other they were probably lovers. The realtor did say there was a small gay community there.

Irene ended up being a lovely Native American woman who would become a living angel to us in many ways. Carol was her disabled husband. She was not a gay woman, but she was the perfect host. Irene came to be one of our greatest supporters and longtime friend on the Eastern Shore.

It was as if she had been waiting for us to arrive. We instantly connected around the subject of rituals and ceremonies.

The fact that we were gay and from up north meant nothing to her. She treated us like her best friends and shared many stories. She promised to introduce us to the people she knew. It was a blessing to meet a person who treated us like family so far from home.

No less than eight hours away from New York City on the Eastern Shore of Virginia, in a rural area just north of the Chesapeake Bay Bridge tunnel, there is an area called Trehernville. It was there we were granted a bank loan to purchase what would become the Rising Spirits Healing and Learning Center on 70 acres of wooded land. This was the place I prepared to settle down for a new life.

Here, I would manifest a dream I had not anticipated until the moment I was invited into it.

Two years prior, Nicole and I agreed to turn our private practice into a nonprofit agency. Rising Spirits Healing and Learning Center Inc. offered services to women and children that encouraged and empowered them to grow and heal. The goal of our organization was to expose women and children to different approaches to healing. We did that by offering training, workshops, and an annual community event called "A Day of Healing and Community." We believed everyone had something to teach and learn, regardless of their age. Bringing elders and children together was quite an honor. Rising Spirits was moving to the Eastern Shore of Virginia.

Anyone who knew Nicole and I knew we were creating learning and healing opportunities for people, particularly women and children and particularly brown and black. Rising Spirits had been Nicole's idea. After we decided to move forward with it, a friend Aiku recommended the Eastern Shore as the home for our new organization. Before moving, Nicole and I traveled to Trehernville several times, visiting the local social service agencies, and sharing our thoughts and plans for the land we had purchased. On one of our visits, we met with the Chairman of the Architectural Department at the local Community College. We had left on cloud nine. We could hardly contain ourselves when he offered to support the project by having the architectural students work on our plans.

We met with the local planning Board of Directors at the courthouse to start the process of obtaining permits to build our retreat space. They gave us a list of tasks to complete before our next hearing date. Prior to getting our permits, we had to meet with neighbors to explore any opposition they might have concerning our project.

With a bit of trepidation, we visited the few neighbors who lived in the vicinity. Most of them were in full support of us building the retreat center. We did get some interesting feedback from a couple of people who said, "People come here today with lots of ideas and plans and leave tomorrow. We never hear from them again."

After our visits, we concluded that some people were not interested, some were distrustful, but the rest seemed hopeful about the idea of us building a retreat center.

We followed the suggestions from the board and prepared to return to the Eastern Shore for our next hearing. We were confident that our permits would be granted this time, and we would soon be on our way to breaking ground. As expected, only a few people joined Nicole, Irene, and me at the courthouse. But within a few minutes—it seemed like a flash—the little courthouse had filled up with people. Seemed like at least a hundred.

I said to Nicole, "I wonder what case is coming up after our hearing? Must be pretty big for this crowd to be here."

I had never seen so many people in one place at the Eastern Shore, not even when we had been there for the community health fair.

We soon realized what was happening. The people gathered to block our efforts to get the necessary building permits to start work on our land.

None of us could believe it. Irene was the most upset.

"How dare they give you girls a hard time. They are so ignorant. Don't they see you're trying to do a good thing?"

She went on to talk about how challenging it was for people on the Eastern Shore to accept change. Then she encouraged us.

"Don't let this discourage you, girls."

Not only was she hurt, but we could also tell she was embarrassed by their behavior.

It turned out that the community had drafted a petition and gotten over one hundred signatures to oppose the permit to build our Summer Camp Healing Retreat. How could this be? No one had expressed any concern or opposition. Something was terribly wrong.

After what seemed like just a few moments, the Board of Supervisors spokesperson stood at the front of the room and said loudly, "This hearing is now adjourned.

Then he turned to us and said, "I suggest you get together with the Pastor of your local parish. They are responsible for organizing this petition. You'll have to set up another day for the follow-up hearing."

People ran for the parking lot, got into their cars, and disappeared into the darkness of the night. Bewildered and highly disappointed, Nicole, Irene, and I went out to the parking lot and approached the church representative to ask for information on how to get in touch with the pastor to set up the recommended meeting.

The individual identified as the church representative met us with resistance and avoidance. We knew then that we were up against a lot more than we had already witnessed.

We returned home to New York filled with disappointment but with a heightened sense of determination. We would meet with the pastor and get to the bottom of this. We would answer all his questions and address his concerns.

We finally met with the pastor and his congregation a few months later. The meeting only happened because Nicole, my sister Zulema who was visiting with us, and I decided to show up for their Sunday morning service. After the service, we asked to meet with the pastor to discuss his concerns. We were invited to stay for a meeting with the pastor and the congregation. We were surprised they wanted to have an impromptu meeting but were finally eager to get a meeting. We agreed to meet.

This turned out to be one of the most devastating gathering of my life. They asked the three of us to sit in the pulpit area. They all sat in the congregation area. They accused us of being witches, said we were part of a cult, involved with drug dealers, and were interested in poisoning them with our so-called healthy foods. They called us Yankees and suggested we return to where we came from. The list went on and on.

They had taken everything they heard about us and our project out of context. They responded from a Christian extremist and racist stereotypical perspective to our desire to promote a healthy vegetarian diet, the use of massage, sacred touch, yoga, and meditation as tools for healing. How someone could demonize campfires and classes on essential oils was beyond me. We only wanted to share what we learned about the power of storytelling to honor our children and elders in the hope of giving them a better future.

I sobbed hysterically through most of the meeting. How dare they question our desire to be of service and promote love for humanity? How dare they judge us without even knowing us and disregard the sacrifice we made to create a place of wellness and healing. Nicole tried to answer their questions while dodging the daggers they fired at us. My sister and I sat there in shock, still not understanding what the hell had just happened.

When we told Irene what happened, she was furious. It enraged her that this was the response of Black people who considered themselves children of God. She prided herself on being a good Christian and knew that there was nothing Christian about their behavior. She pleaded with us not to let this run us off.

"I will do everything I can to support you. God is not going to let you down. It may be hard, but worthwhile things usually are. You mustn't give up!"

We heard rumors over the ensuing months that Nicole and I had been used as pawns—a distraction from a community church scam. Unfortunately, we were in the wrong place at the wrong time, wanting to do a good deed and presenting too much of a threat to the status quo.

Soon after that, we left the Eastern Shore without a building permit. The agenda behind the backlash became clear. One of the deacons at the church had decided to run for political office. He needed an issue that would unite his potential constituents. Becoming a protector of a fearful flock turned out to be advantageous for him. The deacon heard about our intentions and began to instigate fear in the community.

"The board of supervisors doesn't care about what happens in the Black community. If these strangers were trying to take over an area in their community—meaning the White community, they never would have gotten so far.

We gotta stick together and fight for our rights. I promise, if I'm voted into political office, I'll make sure to protect our community."

We had not only shared the ideas for our Healing Center, but we had also shared our newsletters, brochures, and other information that spoke to the work we had proudly done in New York. The truth is you cannot plan for everything. Never did I think we would need to protect ourselves from a Black, Christian deacon. The journey continued.

Irene's love and support were real. We had been blessed with someone we could truly depend on. Filled with doubt and disappointment, we returned to New York. We licked our wounds and tried to regroup. We had been burned and burned badly, but we were going to rise from the ashes and hatch Plan B. With ingenuity and courage, we came up with a plan that would not require a building permit, one that would allow the locals to get to know us.

We were not about to give up the dream. We came up with a new and superb idea. We would purchase a commercial building, open a bookstore and healing center, and get the community to know us. Just a few miles from our property, in a town called Cape Charles, we purchased a commercial, store-front building. Amazingly enough, and to our surprise, we acquired the funding to secure the building.

We could hardly believe our good fortune. We owned a beautiful historical building on a commercial strip in Cape Charles.

We were the first Black-owned business in that district in the town's history. Soon we would have the first retreat center, we told ourselves.

I had no idea what seventy acres of land looked like or what it meant to own it. Two city girls were moving south following their dream.

The day we arrived on the land; we were excited to see the trailer. We were grateful to our Sundance sister Helen, who offered to be there when the trailer was delivered. The trailer had been plopped down on one acre of cleared land in the middle of what seemed like endless woods. We were finally on our land, and the manifestation of our dream was on its way.

As we took in the beauty of the woods, towards the end of the clearing, we noticed a wall. What seemed like a ten-foot wall was the corpses of the many trees that had been cut down. The clearing of the one acre to make room for the trailer and our living space was not at all what we expected. When we asked them to clear the trees, we assumed they would haul them off the property to where they could be used. We forgot to make that small yet critical request.

This all came to light when we asked Helen about the leftover wood.

"Why didn't you tell us about this?" We asked Helen.

"I too was overwhelmed when I came out here and saw what they had done. They reassured me this is what you contracted them to do."

Still, the land was indeed beautiful. Perhaps half a mile off the main road, nestled deep in the woods, at the end of the dirt road, was my new home. My home was a 1970's single-wide trailer. It reminded me of some of the row apartments in Manhattan that I lived in as a child. There was a living room, bathroom, two bedrooms, and a kitchen.

Nicole and I looked at each other and, as if practiced, said simultaneously, "We did it."

We were on our land, the land we had worked so hard to obtain. Every penny earned and those borrowed went into purchasing the land. This was the dream we had been dreaming of for several years.

We set an intention to follow our initial plan of Nicole working in New York and me working on the land and in the store. My year alone, awaiting Nicole's return, was amazing. Working on the land and at the store, I got to know people in the community. I met a local Chiropractor, Dr. Bundick, who hired me as a massage therapist at his practice. I thanked Creator for this. I yearned for human interaction. The occasional visits from Boswell, a local contractor, and Nicole's monthly visits were not enough.

I thought it was odd when Dr. Bundick said to me, "As one of the good old boys, it would be good for you to work at my Chiropractic office. It will put you in good standing with some of the locals."

He was right. I met many locals throughout the year of working out of his office. Some of my experiences were wonderful, and others, well, if it were not for Dr. Bundick and his staff recommending me, these people would have nothing to do with me. It became clear that I was an outsider, Black, and something or someone they were very skeptical about.

Soon, Nicole would be returning to New York. Helen would be returning to her home as well. I would settle into the trailer with Missy and Rudea. Thank God for my two Siberian Huskies, my furry friends.

They would become my primary source of community and companionship. I will forever be thankful to Suesheela for providing me with such loyal friends. This was another of the many gifts from my time at the Satchidananda Ashram - Yogaville.

It was an extraordinarily clear and sunny day. I could see rays of sun coming through the trees in the densely wooded area around me. There were many paths, most leading to other wooded areas.

One path led to the sacred oak tree, which, a few months prior, we dedicated to our Ancestors, on one of our many visits.

There must have been millions of birds chirping at the same time when we did the ritual. The aroma of sweetgrass filled the air reminding me of the Sundance Lakota ceremonies I grew to love. As the gentle wind blew, I could hear the rustling of leaves on the trees. There were fields of dandelions and bright yellow daffodils. I thought this must be what paradise was like. The only thing missing was a stream but the huge oak trees made up for it.

There I was at home with what looked like two little cotton balls. I was brushing and combing out the fur on my dog's body. They had what looked like pounds of coffee grinds on their skin. That is what fleas look like? Suesheela had not told me that those little jokers were filled with fleas. The bonding and caring began.

I figured I must have done some things right. I went from Sundance in Show Low Arizona, to the Satchidananda Ashram – Yogaville - in Buckingham, Virginia, to obtain my Yoga Teacher Certification. I had traveled through the mountains, mesas, and cacti of the deserts of Arizona to the lush, green flowers of Virginia near the James River. And if that wasn't enough, I had two amazing dogs. I thought I had died and gone to heaven. For the first time in my life, I was exactly where I wanted to be, doing exactly what I wanted to do.

Nicole and I had discussed a contractor named Boswell coming out to the land once a week to offer me support clearing the mountain of corpses, the dead trees. Thank God for his generosity and his tractor-trailer. Boswell was an exceedingly kind, older White man. We initially connected with him when we were discussing putting in a driveway. Driving to the trailer down the road to our home after it rained was tricky. I was used to driving in the snow but driving on mud was another thing. He told us our options, one of which was using crushed-up oyster shells to make the road easier to traverse. The oyster shells were the least expensive option, so we went for it. I thought that fishy smell would last forever...

Like many other things we had not anticipated on the Eastern Shore, we had not expected to live with that smell. But Boswell was a good guy and gave us a good deal on creating a drivable path from the main road to the trailer.

I would greet him, "Good morning, Boswell. Can I offer you a cup of coffee?"

Even though I had only recently met him, he was the closest thing to a human friend I had on the Eastern Shore, other than our dear friend Irene. I was always glad to see him.

Working on clearing the mound of dead trees was therapeutic. I would get lost in the bonfire and drag the trees into the fire pit with Boswell's help. I could zone out, go anywhere I wanted to, just as I did at the hanger factory years ago. I could travel back to places that brought me joy and comfort. The dark, scary places were only a distant shadow in my memory. They no longer held power over me but were instead a reminder of where I came from and how fortunate, blessed, and lucky I was to be where I was.

The fire was no joke, and it was a real bonfire. My hair was in a ponytail with a bandana over it. I wore my Levi jeans, yellow construction boots, work gloves, and shades. I looked like someone out of a country movie, except I was a city girl, something I would sometimes forget. It amazed me that it all felt so natural to me, almost as if I had lived this life before.

Boswell would pull down the large pieces of wood with the tractor-trailer, and I would drag them out. I used the chain saw to cut them into manageable pieces.

From the top of his tractor, he would yell, "You have to pull on the starter quickly and with all your strength. Otherwise, it will not start. Remember, you can do anything you put your mind to." He would say, giving back to me what I had told him.

When we stopped for water and rest, he commented on how impressed he was with my ability to work hard.

"For a city girl, you sure are daring. I think you've done this before."

There were times when that stubborn gas saw just would not start. But when it did, I was a wood-cutting fool. I was a natural at that too. I told myself, "Look at you, Miss Thing, acting like a country girl."

They say that fire is the most transformative medicine there is. It teaches you about respect, courage, focus, and intention. The fire would transport me back to the ceremony. I could smell the sage and sweetgrass burning. The memory made me recognize how many trees gave up their lives to manifest our dream.

Sometimes Boswell's yelling would break my reverie, my disassociation. "It's time for a break, young lady."

Immediately, in the absence of the loud hum of the tractor, I became aware of the silence. Boswell had been calling my name for a while. Mesmerized by the work with the fire and trees, I was lost in thought until Boswell yanked me back.

When I finally settled down in the shade, away from the bonfire, I would invite him to join me.

"How about some sandwiches, chips, diet Pepsi and chocolate chip cookies?"

"Sounds good to me, kiddo. You gotta be careful with the fire. It's hazardous and can easily get out of control. You seem to be in your own little world."

"I just can't believe God is so good and that I'm here. How about I get our lunch?"

After lunch, Boswell and I would spend a few more hours pulling trees out of the mound and cutting them down in preparation for burning.

The fire had shades of orange and red with rays of purple. It did not take long for me to drift off into its beautiful colors.

Nicole's monthly visits were magical. We would catch up, share our dreams, perform ceremonies to bless and purify the land. We also honored the spirits that once inhabited the land.

We filled buckets with quartz crystals gifted to us by one of our dear Sundance sisters. Determined to do all we could to manifest our dream, we blessed the land with sacred native medicinal sage known to bring clarity and good energy. We burned sweetgrass, frankincense, and myrrh and sprinkled holy and lavender water on most of the seventy acres. We prayed, chanted, drummed, and danced. We had gotten several spiritual readings, one of which mentioned lynching and murders on the land years prior to our arrival. It was suggested that we set up an altar for our ancestors and provide an offering of flowers, sweets, and food.

Despite all that happened and all that was to unfold later, the experience on the Eastern Shore of Virginia was just as life-giving as it was traumatic. It was the most transcendental experience I've had thus far. To this day, I remember the year I moved there to manifest our dream, a dream that would change my life forever. I did not doubt that things would continue to unfold according to plan. But whose plan? God's or mine?

I had never lived outside of New York City. It was exhilarating to now be living on seventy acres of wooded land with nothing more than my two dogs as companions. I not only came to believe in the incredible power of Spirit, but this was the first time I was conscious of completely leaning into Spirit. I had never experienced such equanimity.

This was my first time living by myself, yet I did not experience loneliness. There I was, eight hours away from what I had always known as home, in the middle of the woods, feeling the safest I had ever felt. I walked through the woods in the middle of the night unafraid of the darkness or of anything else for that matter. I never realized how bright the stars could be or how many filled the sky.

On a full moon night, it was as though the sun was out, shining through the woods. I felt connected to and felt a part of Creator. I will never forget those magical moments. I can unequivocally say that this was the best time of my life.

I realized I could do anything I set my mind to do during that year. Fear was an illusion. Fear's agenda was to slow us down keep us from our greatness and our true selves. I was not afraid.

I felt safe, peaceful, and 100% confident that all was indeed well. I felt held by the Earth and supported by the Universe.

I was no different from the stars, moon, trees, oceans, and the many winged, four-legged, creepy crawlers and stones. The Earth was my mother, the sky my grandfather, and the galaxies were my relatives. I got that we were all related.

Even in the worst times of our lives, we were never alone and were always loved. Life on earth was only a phase of our eternal life. There was no need to fear. Instead, we had lots of opportunities to give in, let go and reconnect.

I did not know how I had gotten so lucky. To this day, I cannot explain it. I guess it had something to do with arriving on the Eastern Shore of Virginia after being at Sundance for three weeks in spiritual ceremony and being surrounded by love. I was then spending a month at the Ashram, immersed in peace and mindfulness. It had to be that that had perfectly prepared me to receive the miracle that it was. Although I would never want to relive the traumatizing experience we came to live, it did not come close to the gifts I received that first year living on the Eastern Shore of Virginia.

Nicole joined me on the Eastern Shore a year later, taking her leap of faith. Fully trusting the Universe, we relied on our latest manifestation, Eastern Lights Books Etcetera, LLC, and my work at Bundick's for our sole source of income. The store opened in the spring. There was the excitement of new birth in the air. We held a Grand Opening made sweet by the beauty of the place. We had dark hardwood floors and an amazing cathedral-like staircase leading to antique cabinetry for books and merchandise display on the second level. Friends and family came from out of town to support us. The locals stopped by to support and see what was going on in their neighborhood. Irene, Marsha, our real estate attorney, a few local merchants, Dr. Bundick's staff, and some of our yoga and massage clients came out.

I offered massages, and taught yoga and meditation classes. Nicole ran the retail store. We sold self-help, interfaith, sacred texts, and other amazing books. We also provided essential oils, herbs, crystals, candles, and incenses—all things related to healing. We were there to stay. We felt fortunate and hopeful that soon the community would come to know us. Our dream had taken all the resources we had and what our creditors offered.

Now it was time to replenish our funds. We knew God would continue to provide for our every need, but it was good to have abundance flowing inward. One of my Guru's slogans was "be good, do good." And in that practice, we believed all else that was good would follow.

I sustained regular clientele at the store while working at Dr. Bundick's office. Sales at the store were slow. We had been advised that it would take at least five to ten years before our store would be financially viable. Although we were willing to wait it out, our creditors could not be put on hold.

If necessary, Nicole and I would get part-time or even full-time work. We realized it would take time for the community to understand what we were offering at the store.

The area's fragmented population was not always open to rapid progress. The town was segregated and divided by race, class, and education. There was also division according to whether you were born there and never left, born there, and left, returned, or newly arrived. Sexual orientation was another divisive category. The upshot of these divisions meant that people were scared, suspicious, and untrusting. The lack of exposure to different cultures made respecting diversity even more challenging, particularly in the Black community. Fostering understanding would require every social, communication, and spiritual tool we possess.

Spring and summer were the best seasons to open a retail or service business on the Eastern Shore. Visitors and tourists explored and spent money. The fact that the store had no central air conditioning or heating was less of an issue. With the ceiling fans going and the front and back door open, you could feel the breeze coming from the bay. There was magic in the air.

As the months went by, we settled into our new life. When the work on the land slowed down, we dedicated more time to the store. Preparing for the winter months became our next big challenge. We anticipated sales going down, and that requests for health-related services would continue at a steady rate or magically increase.

As the flow of guests and tourists slowed to a trickle, so did our retail business. The division of race and class was ever apparent. We heard rumors about us. Folks were trying to figure out who we were and what we were all about.

We heard questions like, "Who are those two women? Are they for real? Will they succeed or end up putting up a "for sale" like many others who fell for the Cape Charles dream?"

Many before us had come and gone. We slowly realized that only the White and affluent made it.

With winter quickly approaching, we needed funds to address the heating situation at the store—time for Plan C, the job hunts. We were fortunate to be able to rely on our multiple skills and professions. Nicole and I tapped into every social service organization on the Eastern Shore. Even with master's degrees, more than thirty years of combined work experience, excellent references, and stellar recommendations, our job search yielded nothing. Our credit cards were soon maxed out, and funds were diminishing.

Sustained by the massages I did at Bundick's, my faithful massage and yoga clients at the store, and lots of prayers, we pushed through. My part-time job at the local hospice organization was a blessing but not enough. It got clear that we were in the wrong place at the wrong time, AGAIN. The memory of the day at the Local Planning Board of Directors meeting returned to me. How many times did we need to be told we were not welcome? We were not Black enough for the Black community nor White enough for the White community.

We were in a group all to ourselves, the come-here gringas, probably gay or hiding something. That meant we had very limited possibilities of getting hired. Neither one of us was considered at the one local hospital where they had openings for social workers. Nicole had dreadlocks; it was suggested that she cut them off to be more acceptable and marketable. I had tattoos and wore a nose ring for non-religious purposes, all of which came up at the hospital group interview.

Every day I lost more sleep, peace, and hope. As the days got shorter and the nights longer, sales diminished some days to nothing. Only seven months since the magical opening day of Eastern Lights Books ect., the building was getting colder and colder. Day after day, we asked ourselves, what are we doing wrong? Where did we go wrong? Why are we sitting in this beautiful building, cold, hungry, and feeling defeated?

Had we not prayed enough and done enough rituals and offerings? Had God played a joke on us? Had the Creator taken us this far to drop us? Perplexed, hurt, and scared, we kept holding on. We were still unsure if it was time to give in and let go.

We began opening the store at six a.m. to get the kerosene heater going, warm up the yoga and massage studio area, and let the fumes dissipate. That was followed by smudging with sage and prayers of gratitude. I wondered what exactly we were giving thanks for.

The yoga class routine was designed to warm students up as quickly as possible. I covered them up with blankets as soon as the class came to an end. My faithful students, the same four to six people, we're dedicated and hopeful.

"Things will get better. The Eastern Shore is an interesting place, but we need people like you and Nicole if things are going to change," they would say.

Around nine a.m., the store opened for retail business. My massage clients began to arrive. Heater going, electric and wool blankets on the table, we created a cozy, comfortable, welcoming massage environment. White cotton gloves on my hands, I was ready to work. Clients said I was good. God knows I threw in all the tricks. There were a few people who really wanted to see us succeed. I would have done five or six massages and taught one yoga class by the end of the day. This I was grateful for.

One evening, I was getting ready to put the electric blankets to rest. I approached the retail area of the store, exhausted and cold. I found Nicole sitting behind the counter wearing her coat, scarf, hat, and gloves. She was cold and tired. I sat down on the beautiful, mahogany hardwood floor. My stomach grumbled. My body ached. The cold of the floor went right through me.

"How were things out here?" I asked her.

"Sita, not one person who was not here for their massage came in today."

I could see her struggling to keep down the tears.

How could this be God's plan for us? We had given all we had. We were financially broke and out of plans and ideas.

"I think I've had it. If this is God's plan for us, it sucks. It's also unfair and crazy." I said, crying.

"Let us lock up and go home. Tomorrow is another day." Nicole said as she came over to hold me and dry my tears.

On the land, we continued to burn wood and tried to make the best of things. By now, we had made a few friends. We occasionally gathered for dinner or chatted and deepened our connection. Irene often came over or invited us over. She was convinced that as people met us, they would fall in love with us. And that they did. We fell in love with some folks too. We created a small, tight-knit community there on the Eastern Shore of Virginia.

On New Year's Eve, a couple of friends came down from New York. Irene, Nicole, and I prepared for our first Inipi, Sweat Lodge ceremony on the land. It was a cool night, and the sky was full of stars. We prayed for clarity, direction, hope, and vision. The grandfather rocks were hot, and our prayers were strong. We just needed to know what God's will was for us.

Inside the lodge, we poured out our prayers and pleas and sang our sacred songs. The lodge was a place to let it all out and shed the tears we had held back for far too long. At a distance, we heard gunfire. This was our first New Year's Eve celebration on the land. We assumed that down South, they fired guns just as up North they released fireworks. For us, there was no other way to bring in the New Year except to be in prayer.

We felt fortunate to have an Inipi where we could come together to pray and ask Creator for guidance. With a sense of peace and tranquility, while reflecting on the lodge experience, we wished each other a healthy, happy, and joyous new year.

The next few days, we stayed on the land. We hung around and told stories, cooked together, and laughed a lot. We reminisced about our times in New York and how we had dreamed about being on our own land doing exactly what we were doing. Many thought we were so brave and powerful for following our dream. Our friends encouraged us to keep going.

"God must have a plan for you. Don't quit before the miracle happens, they say."

That afternoon when I was returning home from work at Dr. Bundicks, I noticed our mailbox on the road leading to our trailer was riddled with bullet holes. With my heart racing and in disbelief, I drove back to the trailer.

Nicole, our friends, and I drove back out to the mailbox. We found bullet casings on the ground all around the box. We realized this was what we heard on New Year's Eve during the Sweat Lodge ceremony. We returned to the trailer and called the authorities. After explaining what we discovered, the police promised to call when they arrived so we could join them out by the mailbox. It was not until one o'clock in the morning the next day when we heard from them.

"You want us to meet you out by the mailbox now?" Nicole asked them.

"Yes, we'd like to discuss the incident involving the gunshots you reported."

"No, not tonight. It's a bit late and dark, and we're already in bed. This will absolutely have to wait till tomorrow." She said.

When she hung up, she turned to me and said, "Hell, I might be from the North, but I've heard and seen too many movies. To go out there in the middle of the night to meet some Trooper to discuss my mailbox being vandalized by gunshots, hell no. They must think we are either crazy or stupid."

That night, we barely slept. Something was terribly wrong. The so-called authorities were inviting us to come out to a crime scene a half-mile down a dark, unlit road at 1:00 am in the morning, which made us more suspicious. We never heard from them again. We reported the crime to the local sheriff's office. They told us this type of crime was not within their jurisdiction. Said it was a Federal Bureau of Investigation issue, as it involved a violation of government property. Identifying the proper reporting source became a deterrent for us to reporting the crime. The last we were told; surveillance cameras were available for cases like these. But apparently, they were all out on loan. We would just need to wait until one became available.

16

Through the Fire

This was not business as usual. For the first time in a long time, we were out of options. Our store was struggling, and our home did not feel secure. We had no illusion that the authorities would help us or keep us safe. Life on the Eastern Shore of Virginia was not what we had dreamt it would be.

Then came the final event, the day that sealed it for us. It was January 15th, the day when both my mother and Martin Luther King, Jr. were born. They say that God has a way of doing for us what we cannot or will not do for ourselves. As had become customary, we had a few friends visiting from out of town. We were hanging out at the trailer watching Civil Rights movies. That afternoon, I was on my way to Bundick's to do a few massages when yet another reality check showed up.

The reality was, we'd moved to an area that was stuck in time— a xenophobic, homophobic, racist, sexist, classist community. It was hard to show up to this world. The situation with our mailbox had never been addressed. We doubted it ever would.

I said my farewells and proceeded down the dirt road, leaving the comfort of our humble abode behind. As I approached the end of our road, where I usually turned onto the state road, I could not believe what I saw.

"Oh my God! These sons-of-bitches."

They had barricaded us in. The six-by-six-foot fence at the end of our road had been pulled out of the ground and placed across the road. There was nowhere to go but back to the trailer. This was something out of the movies. If someone was trying to scare us, they had succeeded. Without taking another breath, I put the car in reverse and stepped on the accelerator. I am not sure if I felt rage or fear as I sped back to the trailer. All I could think of was how unfair this all was—flashbacks of being abused and victimized rolled through my mind. Anger toward whoever was perpetrating these hate crimes filled my body with tension and a burning fire in the pit of my stomach that stormed into my heart. By the time I got to the trailer, I felt like I was going to explode.

"Nicole! You are not going to believe this! They have pulled our fence up and blocked us in! We are not wanted here. I can't do this anymore."

I have no memory of what else I said. I felt like something had snapped inside of me. I lost it. I was raging about why God would let this happen to us. I remember Nicole and our friends trying to calm me down.

At some point, the troopers came to investigate the crime scene. Bullet shell casings were still on the ground from the last incident.

"What's going on here?" One of the officers asked.

Nicole explained what happened that day and the mailbox two weeks prior. She also told them the obstacles we encountered trying to report the matter. As we spoke to the officers, we noticed that our mailbox was gone. Not only had they pulled up the fence, but they had taken our mailbox as well.

The troopers found our mailbox in the woods. They took a few of the bullet casings and moved the fence to the side of the road. They said they would not be able to lift prints off the casings because they were too old. They told us there were no fingerprints on the fence. They stated there was nothing else they could do at the time.

Later, Nicole told me that one of the troopers, the female one, suggested getting a shotgun. If we saw anyone on our property, shoot them, drag them to our trailer and call the police immediately. She told us we would be able to charge them with trespassing. Nicole also told me that the officer warned us to be careful with our dogs.

"These people will kill your mother on Saturday and show up to church on Sunday."

I was disgusted. I felt like throwing up. I remember going back to the trailer, getting something to eat, going to bed, and crying myself to sleep.

They wanted us out of their area and out of their town. We knew they would do whatever it took to get us to leave. We did not deserve such horrible treatment. Had we not sacrificed enough? Had we not shown them that we were just two ordinary women trying to fulfill a dream, a dream that was hurting no one and would have enriched the lives of many?

That was the last night we slept in the trailer. The dream was over. Not only could we not fight what we could not see, but we also were not fighters. My fear and disgust turned into anger and rage, mostly towards myself and God. Nicole's fear turned to action; her main goal was to get us the hell out of there.

The next day after closing the store early, we stopped by Irene's house. She had indeed been our guardian angel.

"I'm so glad you girls stopped by. I have been waiting to hear what happened after the last incident. I have been so concerned. What can I get you? You must be so tired and hungry," she said.

I looked at Irene. Her sweet, soft face that usually filled me with hope and made me feel loved was not doing it today.

"It's going to be okay, my dear. Don't doubt God's eternal love and grace," she said as she gave me a big hug.

I fought the urge to be disrespectful and ungrateful. I wanted so badly to say, "Oh really? This sure does not feel like love and grace, Irene. God is either on something or is out to lunch like so many others around here."

But instead, I said, "Thank you, Irene. I really don't want anything except for a shot of whiskey or something."

I knew she had a small supply of whiskey, wine, and alcohol for special occasions. I really wanted to sleep and wake up when the nightmare was over.

She invited me to lay down as she and Nicole sat down to a cup of coffee. She agreed that returning to the trailer was not a good idea. Between all the stories she had heard of and Nicole's impressions from watching the TV show, Snapped, they were sure we would be killed out there. I honestly did not care. I was on the edge of being suicidal. I was tired, angry, sad, disappointed, and just wanted to disappear from life.

For the next few days, we stayed at Irene's. I did not have it in me to show up and pretend that all was well. I did not want to talk to anyone or be of service. I had nothing to give. I laid in bed and cried, eating, and drinking until I was numb and passed out. I was so angry I could not even stand myself.

Nicole would go to the store, hoping that the sales would pick up. She was such an optimistic dreamer. The more I slept, the more I wanted to sleep.

"Cancel my appointments," I told Nicole. "Tell them I am not feeling well or whatever you feel like telling them. I really don't care."

I was done being humiliated. I was tired of not feeling appreciated and being rejected. And now we feared for our life. This was just not fair. How could God, this so-called God we had prayed to so hard, been obedient to, and trusted in, bring us this far to abandon us? What else did we have to give up, our life?

After a few weeks, I knew the time had come for me to pull it together. Although I mustered the energy to go out and try to make some money, my heart was broken. I had lost all hope, and faith was just a joke. I could not wait to get back to Irene's to get lost in my depression and let myself drop into the darkness that my life had become.

Driving up and down Route 13 South, the main strip, at twenty to forty miles per hour, then fifty or sixty miles per hour, used to bring me joy. I would drive through those big open fields past the farms and empty lots filled with big old trees. I loved being able to see the sunrise and sunsets and the open skies of God's amazing world. It was so magical and filled with possibilities. Life there had felt uncluttered and uncontaminated by skyscrapers, cars, and busy people. But now, it was nothing for me to drive down Route 13 disconnected from my body, my eyes clouded by tears, sometimes screaming until my throat was sore.

I would push on the brakes just to hear them shriek. Sometimes I hoped the person behind me would run into me and end it all. Nicole feared me leaving the trailer and worried if I would return.

Although I could not see it then, Irene was God's love and grace. She comforted Nicole and tried to reassure me all would be well. She told us we could stay at her place for as long as needed. She never asked us for anything in return. She knew we felt defeated. And bless her heart, she also believed God had a miracle in store for us.

After a while, Irene and Nicole came up with an excuse for the madness. Two Northern lesbians of color had crossed the line. This was not about some minor local church bishop trying to position himself. This was about one of the good old boys being disrespected.

Shortly before these criminal incidents on the land had begun, Nicole had an unusual run-in with the local pharmacy owner. There were only two pharmacies on the Eastern Shore, both owned by the same White man for over thirty years. We'd had some cable television work done at the trailer by an African American brother who was a customer at the store. Upon completing some of the work, he was hired for and promising to return the next day, he asked to be paid in advance. We agreed. Why not trust the brother? That is what Nicole thought as she wrote him a check. That was the last time we saw him.

"Ms. Molina-Marshall, this is Jim from the pharmacy. I'm calling about your debt." He sounded hostile and frustrated.

"Beg your pardon, my debt? You must be mistaken. I have no pending debt at the pharmacy." Nicole told him.

We were in debt but not to the local pharmacy.

"I have a bad check of yours, and you must do good by it."

It took a minute, but Nicole figured out what had happened.

The local pharmacist had cashed the check we gave the cable guy. We had put a stop payment on it.

"I'm sorry if you cashed a check for a guy that does cable work. But he did not do right by us, and we put a stop payment on the check. I suggest you get back with him, Mr. Jim." Nicole said.

I heard Nicole tell him why she had stopped payment on the check and how he should not have cashed it, given that he was not a banker. When Nicole hung up the phone, she was furious.

"This White man must be out of his mind, talking about how he did one of mine a favor, how we are alike, good for nothing. How I better stop giving out bad checks and pay my debt, or he would let everyone know not to accept our checks."

Before I could tell her to calm down, the phone rang again. It was Jim.

"Don't you ever hang the phone up on me again, you nigger. You better go back to wherever you came from and bring my money down here tomorrow!"

I guess we did cross the line, the racial line. We never saw Mr. Jim again either.

Nicole and Irene concluded that we were being taught a lesson for messing with one of the area's most respected good old boys. Not only did we not do well on his check, Nicole had hung up on him not once but twice. It made sense that he was furious and either put someone up to scare us, or some loyalist had heard what happened and wanted to teach us a lesson. No matter who or what was behind this, these folks were not joking. The authorities were not getting involved.

Everyone we shared the story with would tell us, "Please be careful. It sounds like you're dealing with some extremely dangerous and angry individuals."

It was time to let it go and regroup. We put the store and the land up for sale and got the hell out of there before we lost our minds and our lives.

Within six months, we started planning our move to the Maryland, DC, Virginia area. We had no interest in returning to New York City. As two well-educated and professional women, we had high hopes of finding work in the DMV.

We made the six-hour trek from Irene's on the Eastern Shore to our friends Carey and Roxanne's in Maryland for job interviews.

"Your properties will sell soon, and you'll get a new start," Carey and Roxanne said, trying to keep our spirits up.

God was not done with us yet. It was not until a couple of years after moving to Maryland that our properties finally sold.

We landed jobs with relative ease and got an apartment in Laurel, Maryland. Nicole and I were hired by the same organization, the DC Child and Family Services Agency.

Although we had a new life and were doing well, my faith had taken a big hit. How does one keep going without hope or faith? I wondered if I would ever get over the disappointment in my heart and hurt in my soul. How could I believe in a God that just kept disappointing me? Why did He allow my mother and father to be such a disappointment, my brother-in-law to be a predator, and my sister to join him?

Why did God let Cesar break my heart? Why was he allowing me to grow old without having the gift of bearing a child? Why would God trick me into believing that I would find peace and joy if I worked hard and served Him and others? Why would He lead us to the Eastern Shore, not once but twice? Why did He open the way, allow us to get so close to our dream, and let it all come crashing down?

I decided God was an illusion for those who could not face life on life's terms. God was a cop-out, along with all the nonsense of spirituality and rituals. These were all false ways of comforting ourselves. The God stuff was for the weak, the dreamer, and those who wanted to live in a fantasy. I decided there was no rhyme or reason to this faith thing. Life is just what it is. You win some; you lose some, you hurt some, you get hurt, you live, and you die. You wake up, work, eat, sleep, and keep doing it repeatedly. None of it makes any sense. There is no purpose and no goal. You make money and spend it and just keep going around and around.

So yes, we had a home, jobs, and each other, but I had lost my way. Maybe I was never really on the journey. What I did know was that I was tired and lonely. For the first time in my life, I felt truly alone.

17

New Directions

No matter how depressed and disgruntled I felt, our new apartment was quite sweet. It was one bedroom with a den and a large balcony. There was a wall-to-ceiling window in the living room facing the east. We got to see the sunrise every morning. We had a beautiful view of the city lights and lots of beautiful treetops. It was a quiet neighborhood and close to all the conveniences. We lived approximately four blocks from the Montpelier Park and Arts Center. They offered everything from free jazz and opera concerts to jewelry-making and ironwork classes.

Recognizing the beauty and gifts we had been given did not come easy for me. Some days I felt like I could barely breathe. My lungs had too much grief to process—I had no more space. It was like a ton of debris laid out on my chest that kept me from feeling anything other than pain. I had an overwhelming need to release. Releasing pain was not new, but I never thought I would experience this kind of pain again.

One day soon, I said the words I needed to say to get free.

Girl, you must release. This is the kind of pain that knocks you down to your knees. Even when you think there is nothing else to release, follow the energy, the breath, the voice. When you think you're feeling sad, when anger comes up, keep following it until you find the rage. When you have exhausted yourself, laughter and joy will show up. Just follow the energy. Trust me on this one. Before you know it, you will be howling, chanting, dancing, laughing, and stomping. And although it might cross your mind that you could just run and get away from it all, keep moving. Give birth to the voices that have been waiting to be released. Complete the journey this time around.

One thing I learned from my experiences on the Eastern Shore is that arriving is only an illusion. We all need a destination point to keep moving. But what are we profoundly moving towards? Where does the ocean end? Does the river ever stop flowing? Pain comes and goes but it never truly stops coming. We must remember that it will go away again when it shows up.

Our home was on a third-floor walkup in a large apartment complex with houses arranged in small clusters. It was quiet and clean. Coming from living in a single-wide trailer in the middle of the woods, this was like being in a five-star hotel. The open floor plan included a huge living and dining room, a large bedroom and walk-in closet, modern appliances, and beautiful oakwood floors and cabinets. But the big prize was the den. Nicole agreed I should go ahead and claim the den.

"You deserve to have your own space to meditate, do your yoga, and continue to heal."

It was perfect, just the space I needed. I used some of my quiet time to engage in adult coloring books. I loved coloring mandalas and yantras, sacred Eastern symbols. I enjoyed organizing the shades of different colors and losing myself for hours in creating kaleidoscope-like drawings. I learned that laying on the floor, listening to sacred Yogic chanting music with my coloring books was great medicine for my mind and spirit.

I even got to the point where I opened a massage table and began to offer friends and family massages. It was only a matter of time before I offered massages almost every weekend and several nights a week. I still had the touch. That is what Carey and Roxanna, our friends from Colombia, Maryland said. It was partly their encouragement that got me to start a small bodywork and therapy practice. The instant peace and clear mind I experienced when I offered massages and energy work kept me doing it.

Despite losing everything and at times feeling like I had lost myself, I still had Nicole. Nicole told me how difficult the transition from the Eastern Shore had been for her.

"I was scared I was going to lose you. We had already lost our dream but to lose my best friend, wife, and dream partner would've been unbearable." Nicole said.

She had been devastated too. The disappointment, fear, and anger she felt toward the people who went out of their way to make sure we left the Eastern Shores had been overwhelming. Years later, Nicole would share that although she was deeply wounded, she had no choice but to shut down her emotions and needs.

"One of us had to pull it together and keep going."

I was grateful to her for holding us down, but at times I resented her for holding onto her faith. This was the start of our relationship challenges. Losing our dream, feeling a daunting distance from each other, burdened our new and magical marriage.

Those first jobs we landed in the District of Colombia were ridiculous. I had sworn never to work for the department of child welfare. No matter the state, the department of child welfare is known to be a tough place to work. The hours are long, and the rewards are minimal. People take jobs with them for the benefits and decent salary. Clients do not see you as child protective agents but instead as the people who come to snatch up their children.

There are way too many hurt, wounded, and violated children to keep track of and even less appropriate homes to place them in. Children get taken from their homes only to end up caught up in a system of organizational and bureaucratic dysfunction. Rarely do they get placed in a safe home, especially as a black and or brown child. I should know...right?

Nicole was hired in the adoption department and had the tough job of finding homes for children waiting to be placed in what was called "their forever families." She worked day and night to find homes for the children and support the families who adopted them.

Lots of the children experienced so much abuse that they were unable to adjust by the time they got adopted. I ended up in the subsidy department. My responsibility was to draft the documentation necessary to assign financial assistance to those adopting children with special needs. At first, I was excited. I looked forward to evaluating the children's physical and emotional challenges and needs. It would not be long before I found out that my work was repetitive and mind-numbing. My job was really to change the names on the pre-written contracts. I was not required to think or assess very much at all. Truth be told, my nine-to-five job could have easily been done in a couple of hours a day.

With a master's degree in social work, a massage therapist license, a yoga teacher, and a Reiki Master certification, and over ten years of experience; how could I have ended up in a job like the one I had. I sat at my desk and cried most of the day. In-between printing and assigning subsidy contracts to adopted children, I poured my disappointment and sadness into a journal. What does one do when all you've ever wanted falls apart? What do you do when your heart is broken? When you have no more hopes, dreams, or desires? When you feel like you have no purpose for living?

Day in and day out, I went to the D.C. Child and Family Services agency. Before noon, I was done with my responsibilities. My supervisor expected me to sit at my desk and pretend I was busy. I had always worked hard and often lost myself in my work. Work kept my mind free of worries and gave me a sense of purpose. The idle time was torture. My mind consistently churned the Eastern

Shore story around and around, that is, when I was not stuck in my childhood memories.

To cope with the depression, I reverted to my Eastern spiritual practices. The Eastern philosophies emphasized that God was not an external thing. God was inside of us. I could no longer trust or believe in God, but I could believe in myself. I could continue to be disappointed and angry at God, or I could move on and reclaim my peace.

At the office, I discovered that no one would miss me if I took a two-hour lunch break instead of an hour or if my fifteen-minute breaks turned into forty-five minutes. I realized others in my department went shopping; got their nails and hair done in the middle of the day. Many went to the LA Fitness gym up the street.

When I got tired of journaling and reading and could not take one more person asking if I was okay, I started leaving the building. After a few months of working there, I had developed my work schedule. The first part of the day, I would journal, read, and complete work responsibilities. By 11:00 a.m. I was ready to go to the gym.

I would stay on the treadmill for sixty to ninety minutes. I tried to run fast and hard enough to make my heartbeat drown my thoughts.

Nothing impressed me much. The agency offered lots of training, but they were either poorly prepared or presented or way below my professional capacity. However, things turned around the day I participated in a training offered by a fellow sister agency.

The organization spoke about children and adoption in a way that touched my heart and reminded me of why I was in the helping profession. Upon completing their moving presentation, they mentioned they were looking to hire a Bilingual Therapist to run a new program. They asked that we help spread the word. Before I knew it, I was expressing interest in the position. A few weeks later, I left the DC Child and family Services Agency and started a job I could grow in. I finally felt the blessings of those six horrible months, working for child welfare,

Designing, developing, and supervising the Lifelines for Kids Program at the Center for Adoption, Support, and Education, Inc. served as a slow rebirthing of my higher self. So many kids had been promised a "forever home," but the trauma, grief, and loss they had experienced had robbed them of the ability to attach to a new family. Initially, the kids were usually ecstatic to have a new home, but their lack of trust got in the way. My job was to help them trust again. I encouraged them to open themselves up to hope and believe again, something I was just beginning to do myself. I found myself developing a program that acknowledged the impact of years of trauma, including multiple losses, disappointments, and heartbreaks.

My heart went out to these kids. All of them had come from dysfunctional homes, parents, or caretakers. Their parents struggled with mental illness, addictions, or lacked the ability to care for their children appropriately. These kids had dreams, many of which went unrealized. Their poor little hearts could only be broken so many times. They learned that the way to protect their heart was not to believe, trust or hope. They had concluded that if they could not depend on their own parents, they could not rely on anyone.

I encouraged them to talk about their losses, the many friends they had left behind, the schools they transitioned from without ever saying goodbye. They also got to grieve the families they connected with but decided not to keep them. They had to learn the rules of a new neighborhood all the time, their place in the chronology of their sibling group, or wonder whether they would see their favorite toy again.

I wondered who they blamed for their misfortunes. Did they blame their parents, the system, or God? Or like me, did they blame themselves for trusting and believing.

My task was to teach them how to restore hope, trust, and for some, to experience it for the first time. I also was tasked to teach them to never give up no matter what. In my heart of hearts, I wanted to tell them, "Don't do to yourself what others have done to you. You will learn to depend on others when you are able to depend on yourself. Learn all you can and strengthen your mind so that disappointments become lessons. And lastly, welcome the opportunities for growth and healing that come your way, even when hurtful."

I developed an exemplar, research-based program for the prevention of adoption disruption. I not only figured out how to teach the kids to keep hoping and dreaming, but I also taught myself.

I started visiting the Ashram more frequently, dedicating time to my yoga practice and spending time just being quiet. I did not allow myself to dwell in the past for too long nor to get too far into the future. I learned to honor the moment and found that the greatest peace I could experience was what I gave to myself; quieting my mind was the beginning of that.

"How would you guys like to learn how to do Yoga and meditate?" I asked some kids I was running a group with one night.

A few seemed interested but most made their knowledge of Yoga clear by saying in unison, "Ommm."

Shortly after that, I added mindfulness and meditation to the curriculum. And when things got out of control, we hit the floor and did some Hatha Yoga.

I often thought about my time at the Ashram and my dream to be a yoga teacher. It was always my desire to bring peace and a sense of safety to others. That was when I got the idea to make teaching Yoga a center point of my primary work. The Eastern Shore was not the right place for my healing center, but I refused to let that experience strip me of my gifts and hard-earned skills.

That night when I got home, I pulled out an old Yoga teacher directory. They had been sending them to me once a year, and I never even looked at them. I was shocked when I saw my name listed with the instructors in Virginia. CanteWi (my Lakota spiritual name) Molina -Integral Yoga Teacher.

So much had happened since my time at the Ashram, where I was filled with joy, hope, and endless possibilities. I had even stopped using my sacred name. I flipped through the directory. I was curious about who was in my area. There were several instructors in Maryland, where I presently lived. Just as I got ready to put the booklet down, I noticed a woman whose name was Pretti Greene in Silver Spring, Maryland.

On my first trip to the Satchidananda Ashram for my teacher training and certification program, I had met Pretti, one of the assistant facilitators.

"If you ever find yourself in the DC/MD/VA area, look me up," she said. I thought that was sweet of her. I shared that I was on my way to the Eastern Shore of Virginia to open a healing center.

I called Pretti the following day. To my surprise, she remembered me.

"You were the student that spoke about starting a healing center somewhere in Virginia. Is that, right?"

I told her the highlights of the Eastern Shores story and that I was now living in Laurel, Maryland. She told me she was looking for a substitute teacher for some yoga classes she taught at Holy Cross Hospital in Silver Spring. I could not believe what I was hearing. Was it possible that I would be subbing for Pretti?

A short while later, I was subbing for Pretti and, in time, was teaching three to four classes per week at Holy Cross Hospital. I could not believe I was getting paid to do something that brought me so much joy. Teaching Yoga was like traveling to a place where all was well—a place where there was nothing to do and nowhere to go. It was a place where we were all safe, and each person got to define their boundaries. I encouraged my students to explore their bodies, relax into their sensations, breathe through the pain, and discover the peace of letting go. It was sacred and auspiciously divine.

Most classes started with an invitation to be present and focus on the possibilities.

"As you sit, let the floor fully support your body. Feel your sit bones reaching for the ground as though you are rooted in the earth. Feel the strength and stability of the ground beneath you. And as you take a deep breath, imagine your lungs filling up with loving energy. Imagine the soft color of a pink rose or liquid gold filling the body. See everything that has or might disturb you being released and transformed. Imagine that for this moment, there are absolutely no worries."

What a gift to see my students surrender to the moment. I felt like I was serving the most amazing beings. It was an honor to help them connect or reconnect with their bodies, mind, and soul and see them get in touch with the divine beings they were and still are. I reminded them that they could either give up or give in and open up. I invited them to be patient, persistent, and consistent. I challenged them to believe they could create their own reality by managing their thoughts and their responses to them. The Yoga experience became a metaphor for life, not just for my clients but also for me.

So much had been lost, but it made my purpose stronger. I was put on earth to serve and assist in the growth and healing of other people. I could not escape my life purpose despite my sadness, disappointment, and fallout with faith.

My students loved and were very appreciative of me. They did not know that they had provided me with the opportunity to reclaim my life.

My students regularly commented on how cared for they felt in my class. "I never had a teacher who was so attentive. It's like you already know what we need, a pillow, a yoga block, belt, or even a blanket to prop ourselves or cover our bodies with when we get cold. You are truly gifted. You not only tend to our bodies, but you also tend to our souls." Some students compared the class to going to a church service. I guess I poured all I had into those opportunities. I was the happiest and most at peace when I was serving others. Through this process, I found healing from the devastating experiences on the Eastern Shore. Through the process of serving others, I found my true purpose for living.

Shortly after I started working at Holy Cross Hospital, I got offered the opportunity to do talks. If teaching Yoga was a gift, doing talks was the grand prize. I did talks on the benefits of meditation, relaxation, and visualization. I developed new talks on the benefits of alternative healing practices and the gift of mindfulness. I became an advocate for how these practices could help heal many ailments and relieve stress. I even taught a course called Laughing Meditation and was tickled to the point of falling out laughing when I realized I got paid to laugh. I explained the benefits of laughter; improving blood circulation, strengthening the respiratory system, massaging the abdominal muscles, and releasing toxins.

I used to carry two stuffed party animal hats I had gotten at a carnival, one for me and one for whoever volunteered to be my assistant. Those talks got me invitations to speak on various other topics I had become knowledgeable about. I never thought sharing my knowledge and enthusiasm about mindfulness, health, and healing, along with topics related to trauma and hope, could become my work.

Three years after starting the Lifelines for Kids Project at the adoption agency, I slowly transitioned from full-time to part-time. Eventually, I got so busy with my own work that I decided to leave the agency and work for myself. My entrepreneurial spirit had been beaten but not killed.

In the meantime, our properties on the Eastern Shore of Virginia sold. We purchased a lovely new home with the space we needed to live comfortably. I created a beautiful Zen-like workspace on the ground level of our home for both work and relaxation. The walls to the yoga studio were a deep rich golden color like what the monks wear. We had lots of pillows sprinkled around the room and purple and black Blackjacks for people to sit comfortably on the floor.

I kept fresh flowers in the space and used scented oil diffusers with the smell of lavender. The treatment rooms where I offered psychotherapeutic massage and psychotherapy were a lighter gold and terracotta color. The furnishings were minimalist yet classy. We used lots of wood and glass and had candles burning throughout.

The lighting was soft and inviting, and the central music dripped sounds of chimes, small bells, and waterfalls. Sometimes I would go downstairs and stretch out on the dark purple and black carpet.

We owned a few porcelain statues of Kwan Yin—the East Asian Goddess of compassion, kindness, and mercy. We also had statues of a Black Jesus, the Buddha, the Egyptian Goddess Nut, various African Orishas, and several Native American symbols. We hung a beautiful, fifty-pound tiled Sunset made for us by a friend and client from the Eastern Shore, on a large open wall. This had served as the front of our counter at the store. That sunset was something we just had to keep.

Though I taught Yoga, I did not mention God often. I believed in goodness, love, and peace and that there was indeed a higher power. I did not need to define or name it. Before going to the Eastern Shore, in my time at the Satchidananda Ashram, I was introduced to the concept of interfaith. Being interfaith meant you believed there were many paths to the Truth but only one Truth. Many faiths but only one Creator.

I had immediately fallen in love with a place called LOTUS, which was an acronym for Light of Truth Universal Shrine. At LOTUS, they honored many different faiths by displaying a beautiful altar for each. I was so taken aback when I noticed they even had a symbol and space for faiths not yet identified.

About a year after leaving the devastatingly disappointing experience of the Eastern Shore of Virginia, I was working full-time for myself. I taught Yoga, meditation, mindfulness skills offered massages, Reiki, and other forms of energy work. I provided psychotherapy and did various training and talks. I even created a CD titled Gentle Yoga with Santa. Me, at a recording studio, who would have thought?

Nicole and I decided to erect a peace pole in our front yard. We invited students, clients, and friends to join us in erecting it. We dug a hole for the Peace Pole and worked together until the concrete was poured and the pole was stabilized. We sang songs of peace and joy and laughed. Then we shared a meal, dialogued, reminisced about the event, and dreamed up the next one. As people departed, each received their own miniature peace pole engraved with the message, may peace prevail on earth in several different languages.

On one of our excursions, we were introduced to a labyrinth. We had the opportunity to walk one that had been painted on canvas. Nicole and I noted that it would be great to have a labyrinth made of stones on our land (our back yard). The day came when a pickup truck delivered a ton of stones to our driveway. The labyrinth was on.

One by one, we laid the stones and created a unique prayer structure. It was perfectly manicured and adorned with plants and flowers in the center. There was just enough space to sit, smudge and meditate before walking out again.

One day more than twenty people came to visit the labyrinth. My spiritual sister, Nazeeha, who had been deemed the queen of the crystal singing bowls and the harp, chanted and played a sweet angelic melody. You could see them from the deck's upper level as they walked the labyrinth. It was so beautiful until a thunderstorm struck, and they had to run back to the house for shelter.

I did not run when the thundering began. Instead, I sat in the center of the labyrinth and let the rain shower me. Others joined me, and we laughed, cried, and screamed at the top of our lungs and stretched out in the mud. It felt like the earth was absorbing what the rain cleansed from us.

This was the beginning of the many spiritual community events we held at the house. We had fire ceremonies, end-of-the-year ceremonies, drumming circles, equinox, and solstice retreats. We even built an Inipi Sweat Lodge. On those amazing days, when I would gather the willows, I would offer prayers and tobacco to every tree whose life I took. Such were the Native ways I learned from my Sundance family. You had to honor the energy you take and only take it if it is life-giving. This was true, particularly when taking from Mother Earth. We conducted solstice and equinox Inipi purification ceremonies for four years, which evolved into our new spiritual community.

After one of our gatherings, it hit us. The dream had been unfolding all along. In a mysterious way, when we no longer cared about it, we supported a spiritual community without expecting it. We offered people the opportunity to come together to heal, love and hope. We created and manifested a healing center. Circle of Light was born!

I remember looking at myself in the mirror and saying: Hey darling, look at you. Look what you dreamed up—freedom to be, love, and be loved—a strong warrior woman. Ground your staff and squat to the earth. You did it. It was you that fought the demons. You that kept pulling me out and guiding me. You who kept the faith and allowed for the dreams of someday being free to come through. Celebrate! Celebrate! Celebrate! Thanks to you, every aspect of yourself that loves you prostrates her body for you. She releases you from this mission of trauma. She is now with you. We are finally one. Now put down your staff and rest, laugh, receive, and celebrate. This work taught me that every aspect of ourselves loves us and thanks us. Our inner selves bows to us, and I was released from my mission of trauma. My authentic self and I were finally one.

I did not want to call it a miracle, but it certainly seemed like one.

During this time, I reflected on the fact that I had been praying all along. I also had been believing and hoping again. I had let God back into my life. I had experienced what I thought was a complete disconnection from God. What I experienced were the steps of reconnecting, accepting, and integrating the transformational power of faith, faith in something greater than anyone God, anyone belief, anyone doctrine or way.

What I had been experiencing was a reclaiming and rebirthing of my unique relationship and understanding of what many call God. Others call it the Great Mystery; some simply call it a higher power or magic.

This thing—God—was too great to be called and experienced as any one thing. My attachment to what I desired, expected, and believed was at the heart of the betrayal and disappointment I experienced. It was the racist, sexist, classist, oppressive human beings that had betrayed, abused, and challenged me, not God.

I became aware that my belief in God was much more encompassing. God is not our benevolent father whose job is to keep us happy, punish us, give, and take from us. God is the universal energy that uses everything for good. God is that which just IS. We must stay present. We must seek, hope for, and find the silver lining in everything and in all things. It is in so doing that we find God. By God, I mean the Universal Energy that lives within all of us.

In this realization, I began to move through the earth as a co-creator and a mature, responsible, multidimensional being.

The End

For Contemplation and Discussion

Dear Reader:

The journey of life can sometimes be devastatingly challenging. If your journey had elements of abuse and violence, the residual damages do not simply disappear. With determination and commitment, we can learn new ways of being. We can find tools that support us in overcoming the seemingly severe, crippling effects of childhood sexual and other forms of abuse.

I have been one of the fortunate survivors. Through Grace and the expert support of therapists and healers of all stripes, I have learned to live with gratitude and hope. Over the years, bit by precious bit, I have managed to create the stable life I once dreamed of, the healthy relationships I cherish, and the career that turned out to be my calling. My deepest desire is to pass that hope to others struggling to have healthy and fulfilling lives.

What follows are a few questions and answers to ponder. Not only about the part of my life contained within these pages but also the parts of my story you resonate with, and that you might want to examine and explore.

Ask yourself the following questions and jot down the answers in a journal or discuss them with your mental health professional or other healing supports.

1. What is trauma, and what constitutes a traumatic event?

Psychological trauma is the unique response or experience to an event in which the individual's ability to process their emotional experience is overwhelmed. This event shows up as something or someone who threatens a person's life, integrity, or sanity.

Trauma is an event or experience that overwhelms the nervous system, or as I call it, the Body, Mind, and Spirit. It renders us incapacitated to re-regulate or un-overwhelm ourselves. Trauma is not about the event but how the individual's nervous system is affected and responds. One of the roles of our nervous system is to protect us by releasing the necessary chemicals in our brain to engage a Fight or Flight response to remain alive. Some of us go into freeze mode and prepare to die, hoping that the threat leaves before we do. This function of going into a sympathetic response, the activated physiological response to run or fight, is supposed to be temporary. If we can successfully resolve the issue, the nervous system can return to its para-sympathetic response, calm, and relaxed state. We can return to normalcy, which looks like a sense of safety, meaning we no longer feel threatened.

Many trauma survivors get stuck in these responses, unable to fight, flight, or freeze themselves back into safety. Instead, they remain stuck with an incomplete trauma response. This is what later creates havoc in their lives.

These incomplete trauma responses become the catalyst for self-medicating, engaging in self-injurious behaviors, and experiencing anxiety, depression, and panic. Many survivors go into autopilot and respond to falsely perceived or real threats triggered by conscious or subconscious memories of abusive incidents. These responses become habitual and create unrelated collateral damage. With therapeutic interventions and healthy, safe social interactions, the body, mind, and spirit, and one's nervous system, can re-regulate itself and return to wholeness.

Reflection questions:
- How is your trauma experience affecting you?
- Do you find yourself habitually responding to real or perceived traumas or triggers with a Fight, Flight, or Freeze response?

2. Is sexual abuse and incest the same thing?

Incest is a form of sexual abuse. Sexual abuse can be defined in many ways. No matter what we call it or how we define it, experiences in which one is forced, manipulated, or otherwise made to have sexual interactions or experiences against one's choice and without consent is sexual abuse.

Incest is defined as forced sexual experiences between relatives by parents, aunts, uncles, grandparents, siblings, and a younger or a less able child. Similarly, childhood sexual abuse can be between student and teacher, coach and mentee, clergy and parishioners, or an authority figure and a minor.

Incest can also happen when a child is exposed to sexual experiences against their will. If there was no consent or the person did not have the freedom or ability to give consent, it is/was abuse.

Sexual abuse can be between known and unknown parties. More frequently than not, the perpetrator is known to the survivor in some way.

Childhood sexual abuse usually includes a power disparity due to age or capability. Consequently, individuals who have been abused by relatives or authority figures do not always consider incest or sexual abuse. Often in these experiences, there can be confusion,

229

guilt, and shame stemming from the perpetrator's psychological or mental abuse, emotional manipulation, and intimidation.

There is also the commonly identified experience of what is called grooming, where the perpetrator, over time, gets the survivor to trust them, depend on them, and ultimately obey their request. Often, the grooming memories and experiences affect and impact the sense of guilt, shame, and misplaced responsibility survivors feel. Survivors wonder if they allowed it, wanted it, or wanted the gifts and favors that were offered in the grooming process, regardless of the demands and solicitations made.

Then there is rape which is a forced sexual interaction that sometimes includes other forms of violent behavior. Rape can be as violent as having multiple perpetrators at once and using objects and weapons.

Reflection questions:
- Do you identify with my childhood sexual abuse story?
- Do you identify as a sexual abuse survivor?
- How would you define your experiences of sexual abuse?
- Were you a victim of grooming?
- Can you forgive or release yourself from what was never your fault?

3. Where does one begin their healing journey?

If you are asking where to begin your healing journey, know that you have already started. There is no proper place or time to begin. As with any issue or concern, the first step is recognizing there is a need, desire, and right to heal. Start your healing process wherever you are and seek support for what is disturbing you right now. Most often, the challenges we face are from unresolved trauma. I have had the privilege and honor of working with survivors for many years. A common psychological condition implies that if you, the survivor, heal and recover your life, then the crime and the traumatic abuse must not have been that bad. Survivors often struggle and wonder whether the healing journey is worth it. They may feel like the journey to healing is too challenging. They cannot take the pain and challenges of re-experiencing it. Even while they are doing the healing work, the everyday challenges can feel overwhelming.

With the help of a psychotherapist and other healing interventions, one begins to understand the impact of sexual abuse and trauma and how it shows up in our lives. The impact often manifests as addictions, depression, phobias, experiences of panic attacks, compulsive and impulsive behavioral patterns, and difficulties with interpersonal and intimate relationships.

Start with being gentle with yourself, honoring your body through expressive movements such as dancing, yoga, running, Tai Chi, and the use of acupuncture, acupressure, massages, Reiki, and nutrition. Engage in activities that help calm your thoughts and spirit, like meditation, affirmations, visualizations, prayer, writing, and other expressive arts.

It is also helpful to identify a therapy or support group. Being with and knowing that other people have similar experiences can be powerful, especially if you hear from people at different stages of their healing.

Reflection questions:
- How and when did you embark on your healing journey?
- What have you found helpful? What gives you hope and empowers you?
- What would you say to someone who is ready to start their journey?

4. How long does it take to heal from sexual abuse?

An accurate, standard answer to this question is impossible. Many factors dictate the time it takes to heal trauma. Every person is unique, and every sexual abuse experience and dysfunctional family system is different. However, some factors can affect the healing journey.

Reflection questions:
Basic Truths
- Your age at the time of the event(s).
- Whether you told someone, the degree of support you received, and whether you were believed.
- If there were multiple forms of abuse at once.
- If you could get away from the perpetrator(s) and find a safe space.

5. What is the most critical aspect of healing?

Resources and access to services play a critical role in healing. Do not be afraid to seek support, both traditional and non-traditional. Find resources that encourage and guide you to address not just your thoughts but your body and spirit. In my case, I started with talk therapy. After scratching the surface of my trauma in therapy, I explored many other different healing modalities. Each one bought me closer to the return of my true self.

Many believe the process of healing from sexual abuse occurs in stages and in a linear fashion. What I have discovered from my healing journey and hundreds of survivors I have worked with is that the journey is different for each person. Many of us have in common the desire and fear to tell the story of what happened and the immense degree of shame, self-blame, and anger for (believing that we allowed it) allowing it. It is important to note that we did not allow anything. We were victimized. We were victims. And when we start the healing process, we become survivors.

The healing process often moves as a circular experience where you revisit some of the same issues and behaviors. As time goes on, the experiences become more and more distant from the impact of the trauma, less overwhelming. We develop greater capacity and tolerance for what was once intolerable. This makes it possible to address areas that were either not available before or too scary to visit and explore.

Reflection questions:
- How long have you been on your healing journey?
- What therapies, rituals, and practices have you explored?
- What has been your experience with healing?

6. What does it mean if a reader identifies strongly with some parts of this story but not others?

It only speaks to the truth that in some ways, we are exactly alike, but in other ways, we are entirely different. Our experiences are indeed unique and affect us in specific ways. What is critical is to honor our own experiences and story.

Do not minimize, compare, or judge your experience. Reflect on the critical moments in your life and tell your own story. Although the events and situations are different, remember that pain is pain, and how you experience it and the impact it has on you is what matters.

Reflection questions:
- What memoir would your body, mind, and spirit write?
- Have you been afraid of sharing your experience for fear that others may think it is not real trauma?
- Have you minimized or denied your own hurt?

233

7. Many of my friends and family believed I should not talk about my childhood sexual abuse. They said it had been too long since it took place. They suggested I consider how it would affect my family. Many survivors struggle with the question: Should I or shouldn't I disclose or share my secret?

Decisions around disclosure are very personal. This can be assessed by the survivor with the support of an experienced counselor or healer. More important than whether one should disclose or not disclose, is, the question of when and to whom and for what purpose. It is always risky to admit that you have been sexually abused. You want to consider whether your confidentiality will be honored, whether the people you share it with will offer support or judgment, and whether you will be believed. It is also recommended not to disclose with the expectation that the perpetrator will apologize or ever ask for forgiveness.

Disclosing is about breaking the silence, no longer holding the paralyzing and shameful secret of what was done to you. Many survivors keep the secret for years, sometimes having no pre-verbal memories of what took place and other times unconsciously repressing and denying the memories. Sometimes remembering can be overwhelming.

Often disclosure occurs when the perpetrator no longer has power over or access to the survivor when they die or become incapacitated or are disarmed and disempowered. Disclosing supports the healing journey. In that moment, the survivor begins to address their needs and concerns above other people's needs. It is not necessary to disclose to family and friends. Still, it is suggested to reveal at least to a trusted friend, a mental health professional, healer, or in a group of other survivors.

Reflection questions:
- What are your thoughts about sharing your sexual abuse experiences with others?
- If you have a sexual abuse history, have you shared your experience with your family?
- What was their response?

8. Sometimes, when one begins the healing process, one will see, hear, and feel like they are back at the scene of the sexual abuse. Survivors might ask how they can get rid of these experiences? They are unpredictable and vary in intensity.

These experiences are often referred to as triggers and flashbacks that are sudden and disturbing vivid memories of events in the past that are the consequence of psychological trauma. They are challenging to deal with. They can be triggered at any time and by multiple different sources. The memories feel very real and often come with body memories as well. In the ideal situation, a survivor is self-aware enough to track or notice when the trigger experience is coming on. This can allow time to get centered and orient back to the here and now.

Somatic healing techniques teach survivors to focus on something that serves as a resource to calm the activated nervous system in response to the threat. This could look like calling or talking to someone who knows you and can help you calm down. Using scents, textures, extreme temperatures-particularly cold water or ice, brushing the skin, and having affirmations or statements written that can be read as a reminder that you are presently safe. Using images and symbols that break the connection with old abusive experiences or calling on a memory where you have felt safe are only some ways of resourcing. Working with a somatic or mindful therapist engaging in bodywork and physical activities such as dancing, yoga, running, etc., can help manage the activation that provokes triggers and flashbacks.

Reflection questions:
- Do you believe you have been experiencing triggers or flashbacks?
- Have you identified practices that are particularly helpful?
- Can you identify or anticipate when you are getting activated, when having a trigger or flashback?

9. How should you respond if you hear that a friend or family member has been abused?

Becoming aware that someone you love has been abused can be difficult. The most important thing is to make sure that they are presently safe. Let them know that you are there to support them and honor their story. Critical to this question is the age of the survivor. As adults, we are mandated reporters and must do all we can to keep children safe. This is a delicate situation and getting support from a professional can be helpful. Children have a right to their privacy also. We must seek out and find a way to keep them safe while honoring their needs.

However, if this is an adult, remember that it is their story to share when and if they wish. Be there to support them, encourage, and share resources. You might ask, what if they share it with you and ask that you not tell anyone? Be patient and compassionate. Sexual abuse is a crime of shame and violation and is highly stigmatizing.

Hence, be very mindful not to take the survivor's power away by making them feel forced to tell or pursue support and healing. Reporting a sex crime to the police or sharing it with others is not easy and sometimes is not the most helpful to the survivor. The survivor may still be in a relationship with or in proximity to or dependent on the abusive person. Again, your job is to be there when the survivor is ready to share their story and move to the next stage.

Reflection questions:
- What would you do if a friend told you they were sexually abused?
- How would you respond if that friend were a young person?
- What would you want and expect from your friend if you shared experiences of being sexually abused?

10. How is the impact of growing up in a dysfunctional family defined?

A broad definition of a dysfunctional family is a family in which conflict, inappropriate, and often child neglect and abuse occur continuously and regularly, leading other family members to adapt to such actions. In some families, the dysfunctional family system stems from parental figures being physically, mentally, or emotionally ill and children taking on misplaced/reversed roles. It can also be an environment where children experience constant moves, losses, and are witnesses to traumatic events. The conditions of dysfunctional family dynamics are endless; bottom-line, children do not get "good enough parenting and appropriate support, love, and guidance."

In my case, from an early age, there were many factors that pointed to not having the necessary tools or support to function as a family. We were displaced and separated due to our migration to the U.S; whatever mechanisms we used to deal with stressors and issues in the Dominican Republic disappeared once we got to America. My mother was plagued with undiagnosed depression, which led to role reversal. My father was an alcoholic and depended on his anger and rage to gain a sense of control of what was out of his control in our household.

He struggled with adjusting to changes in status, economic stability, and familiarity, all of which affected his view of manhood. My siblings struggled with the effects of mental illness, drug and alcohol abuse.

And the primary family model for addressing emotions and dealing with conflict was through physical, emotional, and verbal abuse and addictions; anything to alter the mood and behaviors.

Growing up in a dysfunctional family not only forces family members to adjust their behavior to deal with and respond to dysfunctional norms, but it also leads to a normalization of dysfunctional ways of being. Situations and events that would not be acceptable in an intact and functional family system go unnoticed in a dysfunctional one. These systems are fertile soil for all types of traumatic events to take place.

Unhealthy attachments, dependency, unrealistic interpersonal expectations support the sustaining of the dysfunctional system; unfortunately, these learned behaviors are passed down to future generations creating generational dysfunctional family systems in which the same or similar maladaptive behaviors are recreated. By embarking on your own healing journey, you release the past and develop new systems for future generations that are free of violence, neglect, and abuse. Psychological patterns that reinforce ill family systems are broken. There are healthy environments where adults and children have age-appropriate roles and responsibilities that support and promote a loving environment.

Reflection questions:
- Did you grow up in a dysfunctional family system? If so, how has it affected you?

- How would you define your dysfunctional family?
- What challenges were you left with, and what changes have you already made or are willing to make to create a functional, loving, and joyful life?

11. How does being an immigrant influence the potential of being sexually abused?

Unfortunately, sexual abuse and violence are an epidemic across the globe. In the United States, 1 in 3 girls and 1 in 6 boys are sexually abused every hour. These numbers only account for the crimes that get reported to the authorities. No one is exempt from the danger of sexual abuse, incest, sexual violence, or physical abuse. Being an immigrant adds a layer of vulnerability, especially in countries where sexism and patriarchy are a way of life – most of the world.

I firmly believe that my immigrant status and the experiences of my immigrant parents and siblings heavily contributed to the worsening of our dysfunctional family system. It was fertile ground for sexual abuse to take place.

My parents and family were separated when I was three years old, at an extremely critical age of the emotional development of a young child. My parents were financially affected, my father struggled to seek employment. He had to adjust to not speaking the language and had little to no emotional and financial support from anyone.

When we finally reunited in the U.S., we struggled through multiple moves, cultural changes, barriers connected to language, and never feeling like we belonged. My mother, until her death, regretted ever leaving the Dominican Republic. I am glad I eventually in my adult life got to return to my birth country.

My parents were not financially or emotionally established enough to provide my siblings or me with the opportunity to reconnect and reacquaint ourselves with our homeland.

Reflection questions:
- Do you come from an immigrant family?
- What was your family's experience migrating to the U.S.?
- Did you ever feel like you did not or do not belong here?
- Did your immigrant story affect your family and contribute to your dysfunctional family system?
- What were the stressors that particularly affected your family?

12. There is a lot of God and mention of spirit in my memoir. You might ask, must one believe in God or belong to a particular faith to heal?

Absolutely not. What is important is to believe in someone or something greater than you, a force you can turn to when you are out of options. A higher power or source that keeps you hoping and seeking a better tomorrow.

I identified with a higher power that I referred to as Mother, Father, God, Spirit, and the Creator of all.

My belief system gave me the strength to endure my experiences and keep moving forward. I believed in whatever helped me feel better, even if it was my own illusion. I have had my issues with God throughout my life.

There were times I could not understand why a so-called omnipotent and omnipresent God would allow such unfair, unexplainable, disheartening, and evil events to occur. But throughout the years, through all the darkness, I realized that God, the Creator, the universal energy was not responsible for the evil, outrageous, and devastating occurrences humans did. God could, however, be credited with the hope that kept me going when I felt beat down and defeated by life

Reflection questions:
- What keeps you moving forward and hoping for a better tomorrow?
- Do you identify with a higher power greater than yourself?

13. What can I expect from working with a Licensed Clinical Social Worker who considers themselves a Holistic/Integrative Psychotherapist?

The word holistic implies whole, complete, comprehensive, or as I like to define it, inclusive of energetic, physical, and subtle, mind, spirit, and all living things.

Consequently, it would be accurate to say that healers, body and energy therapists, psychotherapists, doctors, shamans, and others that practice Holistic Medicine, would probably define holistic therapy according to what they include in their practices.

My definition of Holistic Psychotherapy has evolved over time. As my understanding of the impact of abuse, neglect, and trauma grew, so did my understanding of what it takes to heal. This solidified my commitment to my healing and to discover, educate and prepare myself to serve those seeking support.

It started with the mental, behavioral, and psychological training I received during my clinical studies in social work school and later in clinical post-graduate training. Shortly thereafter, I became interested in bodywork. It became clear to me that the body held memories that the mind had forgotten or perhaps has never been able to process, witness, or tolerate acknowledging. This awareness led to my interest in and dedication to bodywork and massage therapy. I started incorporating what I then called Psycho-Therapeutic Bodywork, a process-oriented physical massage.

During this time, I studied and included other medicinal and healing approaches in my practice. I found that including essential oils and aromatherapy in the treatment for some provided grounding, calming, clarity, detoxification, and even access to memories that would not otherwise be experienced on a verbal/psychological level. I started exploring practices that spoke of energy. This included taking courses in Foot Reflexology, Chakra healing, Safe Touch, and becoming a Reiki Master.

I also developed my Yoga Practice. I taught Level I Yoga, Meditation, and Breathing exercises. My time at the Ashram resulted in obtaining a Teacher Training Certification which prepared me to teach classes. I also learned how yoga supports mind, body, and spiritual wellbeing. And most excitedly, to identify poses that would help the healing of survivors' sexual trauma. Soon after, I added education on the use of medicinal herbs.

These suggestions became essential to those seeking non-pharmaceutical interventions to address issues of depression, anxiety, panic, sleep challenges, irritability, anger, dissociation, lack of energy, and even indigestion and inflammation, to name a few.

There are times when I talk to clients about their beliefs, spirituality, and even religion. I invite clients to create their unique healing experience.

I often say, "My commitment is to offer you a safe place to heal and to introduce you to as many options as possible." Providing clients with Holistic Psychotherapy includes safe touch, Reiki, somatic experiencing, Hatha Yoga, meditation, breathing exercises, visualization, guided imagery, aromatherapy, herbal medicine, and spirituality. We choose modalities as needed based on the client's interests and needs.

Clearly, not everything is for everyone but being able to offer clients different options and hope has enriched their wellness experience, as well as mine.

My clinical practice is my next personal healing level, one in which I get to affirm that healing from sexual trauma is possible. I know this for sure because I have continued to heal from my experiences. What at one point took my life away has given me and many others our lives back. This work continues to provide me with a purpose to live and thrive.

Holistic Psychotherapy is a process by which clients are offered an array of healing practices to obtain wholeness and wellbeing. It provides the necessary tools to continue, forever, their healing journey. This metaphorical flashlight is sufficient to help them stop RUNNING THROUGH DARKNESS.

The paradox of trauma is that it has both the power to destroy and the power to transform and resurrect.

~Peter A. Levine

A Final Note

It has been a privilege spending this time with you. If you'd like to share your experience, thoughts, or comments, reach out to me at: hpbysanta@gmail.com

My hope is that this book has allowed you to further your healing. Should you wish to continue this journey with me, I am excited to invite you to the Trauma to Triumph community. Join here: http://traumatotriumph.net

I look forward to supporting you as you step into your greatest life experience.

Reflections

Made in the USA
Middletown, DE
15 May 2022

65631974R00158